HARRAP'S

French phrasebook

Lola Busuttil

Valerie Grundy

W0010377

McGraw·Hill

New York Chicago San Francisco Lisbon London Madrid Mexico City
Milan New Delhi San Juan Seoul Singapore Sydney Toronto

Copyright © 2006 by Chambers Harrap Publishers Ltd. All rights reserved.
Printed in Singapore by Tien Wah Press. Except as permitted under the
United States Copyright Act of 1976, no part of this publication may be
reproduced or distributed in any form or by any means, or stored in a
database or retrieval system, without the prior written permission of the
publisher.

ISBN 0-07-146746-7

McGraw-Hill books are available at special quantity discounts to use as
premiums and sales promotions, or for use in corporate training programs.
For more information, please write to the Director of Special Sales,
Professional Publishing, McGraw-Hill, Two Penn Plaza, New York, NY
10121-2298. Or contact your local bookstore.

Editor & Project Manager
Anna Stevenson

Publishing Manager
Patrick White

Prepress
Susan Lawrie
Vienna Leigh

CONTENTS

INTRODUCTION

This brand new English-French phrasebook from Harrap is ideal for anyone wishing to try out their foreign language skills while travelling abroad. The information is practical and clearly presented, helping you to overcome the language barrier and mix with the locals.

Each section features a list of useful words and a selection of common phrases: some of these you will read or hear, while others will help you to express yourself. The simple phonetic transcription system, specifically designed for English speakers, ensures that you will always make yourself understood.

The book also includes a mini bilingual dictionary of around 4,500 words, so that more adventurous users can build on the basic structures and engage in more complex conversations.

Concise information on local culture and customs is provided, along with practical tips to save you time. After all, you're on holiday – time to relax and enjoy yourself! There is also a food and drink glossary to help you make sense of menus, and ensure that you don't miss out on any of the national or regional specialities.

Remember that any effort you make will be appreciated. So don't be shy – have a go!

ABBREVIATIONS USED IN THIS GUIDE

adj	adjective	*n*	noun
adv	adverb	*pl*	plural
f	feminine	*prep*	preposition
fpl	feminine plural	*pron*	pronoun
m	masculine	*sing*	singular
mf	both masculine and feminine eg artiste *mf*		
m,f	masculine form and feminine ending eg débutant(e) *m,f*		
mpl	masculine plural	*v*	verb

PRONUNCIATION

Every phrase given in French in this guide is followed by its pronunciation, shown in italics. You just need to pronounce the phrase in the way shown in the simple phonetic transcription in order to make yourself understood by a French person. You don't need to worry about which part of a word to stress. Unlike English, French does not stress any particular syllable. And don't hesitate to ask a French person to show you how to pronounce any sounds you find difficult!

The main thing that makes French sound so different to English speakers is the use of nasalization. This refers to sounds that are produced more through the nose than the mouth. We have used the following two codes to show these:

ON For the nasalized sounds **on**, **en**, **em**, **an** and **am** and a few other combinations in French. Try saying the English word "gong" and stopping short of pronouncing the full "ng" sound. Examples : **montre** *mONtr*, **entrée** *ON-tray*, **flan** *flON*, **ambassade** *ON-ba-sad*

AN For the nasalized sounds **un** and **in** and a few other combinations in French. Try saying the English word "van" and stopping just short of pronouncing the "n". Examples: **quelqu'un** *kel-kAN*, **coussin** *koo-sAN*

The following code transcribes the French **u** sound:

U To pronounce the "u" in French, try pursing your lips as if you were going to say "oo" and then, keeping them like that, trying to say "ee". Note that it is the written French **ou** that is pronounced simply as "oo". Examples: **bus** *bUs* – as opposed to – **route** *root*

Note also the following transcriptions:

ey Used to show the pronunciation of **-eil** and **-eille**, rather as in English "survey" but slightly pronouncing the "ee" sound of the "y" at the end. Examples: **bouteille** *boo-tey*

oy Used to show the pronunciation of the combination **-euil** rather as in English "boy" but slightly pronouncing the "ee" sound of the "y" at the end. Examples: **fauteuil** *fau-toy*

uh Used to show the pronunciation of **e**, **eu** and some other combinations in certain words. Examples: **le** *luh*, **feu** *fuh*, **œuf** *uhf*.

zh   Used to show the pronunciation of **j** and soft **g**. This is exactly the sound of the "s" in the English word "measure". Examples: **j**aloux *zha-loo*, na**g**er *na-zhay*

Some consonants are pronounced differently in French. Here is a guide to these along with their pronunciation:

h   not aspirated in French   Example: **h**abiter *a-bee-tay*
qu   k   Example: **qu**ai *kay*
r   the "r" in French is vibrated at the back of your palate rather than against the teeth as in English
w   v   Example: **w**agon *va-gON*

Pronouncing accented vowels:

à, **â**   *a* (as in English "cat")
é   *ay* (as in English "pay")
è, **ê**   *e* (as in English "pet")

A few common French word endings and how to pronounce them:

-at   *-ah*
-eau   *-oh*
-et   *-ay*
-ez   *-ay*
-ot   *-oh*

Note also that the "**s**" plural ending is not usually pronounced in French: Example: **chats** *sha*

Alphabet

How to pronounce the letters of the alphabet in French when you are spelling a word :

a	*ah*	**j**	*zhee*	**s**	*ess*
b	*bay*	**k**	*ka*	**t**	*tay*
c	*say*	**l**	*el*	**u**	*U*
d	*day*	**m**	*em*	**v**	*vay*
e	*uh*	**n**	*en*	**w**	*doo-bluh-vay*
f	*ef*	**o**	*oh*	**x**	*eeks*
g	*zhay*	**p**	*pay*	**y**	*ee grek*
h	*ash*	**q**	*kU*	**z**	*zed*
i	*ee*	**r**	*er*		

EVERYDAY CONVERSATION

In France, relations between people who do not know one another well tend to be fairly formal. There are two ways of saying "you" in French: the informal **tu** and the formal **vous**. **Tu** is used when speaking to one person you know well. **Vous** is used in formal or professional situations, and with people you don't know, such as sales assistants and waiting staff. If in doubt, you should always use the **vous** form, which is used to address one person or more than one. Note, however, that **vous** is also the plural form of **tu**, used when you are addressing more than one person you know well, for instance a group of friends.

When greeting people, **bonjour** (hello) is used during the day. **Bonsoir** (good evening) can be used from late afternoon onwards and may be used when arriving or leaving. **Bonne nuit** (goodnight) is only used before going to bed.

The basics

bye	au revoir *oh ruh-vwar*, (informal) **salut** *sa-lU*
excuse me	excusez-moi *eks-kUsay-mwa*
good afternoon	bonjour *bON-zhoor*
goodbye	au revoir *oh ruh-vwar*
good evening	bonsoir *bON-swar*
good morning	bonjour *bON-zhoor*
goodnight	bonne nuit *bon nwee*
hello	bonjour *bON-zhoor*
hi	bonjour *bON-zhoor*, (informal) **salut** *sa-lU*
no	non *nON*
OK	d'accord *da-kor*, (informal) **ok** *okay*
please	(informal) **s'il te plaît** *seel tuh play*, (polite or plural) **s'il vous plaît** *seel voo play*

| thanks, thank you | merci *mer-see* |
| yes | oui *wee* |

Expressing yourself

I'd like ...
je voudrais .../j'aimerais ...
zhuh voo-dray .../zhay-muh-ray ...

we'd like ...
nous voudrions .../nous aimerions ...
noo voo-dree-yON .../nooz ay-muh-ree-yON ...

do you want ...?
est-ce que vous voulez ... ?
ess-kuh voo voo-lay ... ?

do you have ...?
est-ce que vous auriez ... ?
ess-kuh vooz ohr-yay ... ?

is there a ...?
est-ce qu'il y a un/une ... ?
ess-keel ya AN/Un ... ?

are there any ...?
est-ce qu'il y a des ... ?
ess-keel ya day ... ?

how ...?
comment ... ?
koh-mON ... ?

why ...?
pourquoi ... ?
poor-kwa ... ?

when ...?
quand ... ?
kON ... ?

what ...?
qu'est-ce que ... ?
kess-kuh ... ?

where is ...?
où est ... ?
oo ay ... ?

where are ...?
où sont ... ?
oo sON ... ?

how much is it?
c'est combien ?
say kON-byAN ?

what is it?
qu'est-ce que c'est ?
kess-kuh say ?

do you speak English?
est-ce que vous parlez anglais ?
ess-kuh voo par-lay ON-glay ?

where are the toilets, please?
s'il vous plaît, où sont les toilettes ?
seel voo play, oo sON lay twa-let ?

how are you? *(informal)*
comment vas-tu ?
koh-mON va-tU ?

how are you? *(polite or plural)*
comment allez-vous ?
koh-mONt a-lay-voo ?

fine, thanks
bien, merci
byAN, mer-see

thanks very much
merci beaucoup
mer-see boh-koo

no, thanks
non merci
nON mer-see

yes, please
oui, merci
wee, mer-see

you're welcome
il n'y a pas de quoi
eel nya pa duh kwa

see you later
à tout à l'heure
a toot a luhr

I'm sorry
je suis désolé
zhuh swee day-zoh-lay

Understanding

attention	warning
entrée	entrance
gratuit	free
hors service	out of order
interdiction de …	do not …
ouvert	open
réservé	reserved
sortie	exit
stationnement interdit	no parking
toilettes	toilets

il y a …
there's/there are …

bienvenue
welcome

est-ce que ça vous dérange si … ?
do you mind if …?

un instant, s'il vous plaît
one moment, please

asseyez-vous, je vous en prie
please take a seat

PROBLEMS UNDERSTANDING FRENCH

Expressing yourself

pardon?
pardon ?
par-dON ?

what?
quoi ?
kwa ?

could you repeat that, please?
vous pouvez répéter ?
voo poo-vay ray-pay-tay ?

could you speak more slowly?
est-ce que vous pourriez parler plus lentement ?
ess-kuh voo poor-yay par-lay plU lON-tuh-mON ?

I don't understand
je ne comprends pas
zhuh nuh kON-prON pa

I understand a little French
je comprends un peu le français
zhuh kON-prON AN puh luh frON-say

I can understand French but I can't speak it
je comprends le français mais je ne le parle pas
zhuh kON-prON luh frON-say may zhuh nuh luh parl pa

I hardly speak any French
je parle à peine français
zhuh parl a pen frON-say

do you speak English?
est-ce que vous parlez anglais ?
ess-kuh voo par-lay ON-glay ?

how do you say ... in French?
comment dit-on ... en français ?
koh-mON deet ON ... ON frON-say ?

how do you spell it?
comment ça s'écrit ?
koh-mON sa say-kree ?

what's that called in French?
comment ça s'appelle en français ?
koh-mON sa sa-pel ON frON-say ?

could you write it down for me?
est-ce que vous pourriez me l'écrire ?
ess-kuh voo poor-yay muh lay-kreer ?

Understanding

est-ce que vous comprenez le français ?
do you understand French?

je vais vous l'écrire
I'll write it down for you

ça veut dire ...
it means ...

c'est une sorte de ...
it's a kind of ...

SPEAKING ABOUT THE LANGUAGE

Expressing yourself

I learned a few words from my phrasebook
j'ai appris quelques mots dans un guide de conversation
zhay a-pree kel-kuh moh dONz AN geed duh kON-ver-sas-yON

I did it at school but I've forgotten everything
j'en ai fait à l'école mais j'ai tout oublié
zhON ay fayt a lay-kol may zhay toot oo-blee-yay

I can just about get by
je me débrouille à peu près
zhuh muh day-broo-ee a puh pray

I hardly know two words
je connais à peine quelques mots
zhu koh-nay a pen kel-kuh moh

I find French a difficult language
je trouve que le français est une langue difficile
zhuh troov kuh luh frON-say ayt Un lONg dee-fee-seel

I know the basics but no more than that
je connais les bases mais pas plus
zuh koh-nay lay baz may pa plUs

people speak too quickly for me
les gens parlent trop vite
lay zhON parl troh veet

Understanding

vous avez un bon accent
you have a good accent

vous parlez très bien le français
you speak very good French

ASKING THE WAY

Expressing yourself

excuse me, can you tell me where … is, please?
excusez-moi, pourriez-vous me dire où est … ?
ek-skU-zay-mwa, poor-yay-voo muh deer oo ay … ?

which way is it to …?
…, c'est par où ?
…, say par oo ?

can you tell me how to get to …?
pourriez-vous m'indiquer comment aller à … ?
poor-yay-voo mAN-dee-kay koh-mON alay a … ?

is there a … near here?
y a-t-il un/une … près d'ici ?
ya-teel AN/Un … pray dee-see ?

could you show me on the map?
pourriez-vous me montrer sur la carte ?
poor-yay voo muh mON-tray sUr la kart ?

is there a map of the town somewhere?
y a-t-il un plan de la ville quelque part ?
ya-teel AN plON duh la veel kel-kuh par ?

is it far?
c'est loin ?
say lwAN ?

I'm looking for …
je cherche …
zhuh shersh …

I'm lost
je suis perdu
zhuh swee per-dU

12

Understanding

allez/continuez tout droit
go/carry on straight ahead

tournez à gauche/à droite
turn left/right

descendez/montez jusqu'à …
go up/down until you get to …

vous êtes à pied ?
are you on foot?

c'est à cinq minutes en voiture
it's five minutes away by car

c'est la première/deuxième/troisième à gauche
it's the first/second/third on the left

tournez à droite au rond-point
turn right at the roundabout

tournez à gauche quand vous arrivez à la banque
turn left at the bank

prenez la prochaine sortie
take the next exit

ce n'est pas loin
it's not far

c'est à deux pas d'ici
it's just round the corner

EVERYDAY CONVERSATION

GETTING TO KNOW PEOPLE

When meeting up with or being introduced to somebody in France, there is always a form of greeting. With people you don't know or between men, the custom is to shake hands. People who know each other well kiss each other on the cheek (**faire la bise**) when they meet. The number of kisses varies between two and four, according to the region.

The basics

bad	mauvais *moh-vay*
beautiful	beau *boh*
boring	ennuyeux *ON-nwee-yuh*
cheap	pas cher *pa sher*
expensive	cher *sher*
good	bon *bON*
great	génial *zhay-nyal*
interesting	intéressant *AN-tay-re-sON*
nice	*(good)* bon *bON*, *(pretty)* joli *zhoh-lee*, *(kind)* gentil *zhON-tee*
not bad	pas mal *pa mal*
well	bien *byAN*
to hate	détester *day-tes-tay*
to like	bien aimer *byANn ay-may*
to love	adorer *ah-doh-ray*

14

INTRODUCING YOURSELF AND FINDING OUT ABOUT OTHER PEOPLE

Expressing yourself

my name's …
je m'appelle …
zhuh ma-pel …

what's your name?
comment vous vous appelez ?
koh-mON voo vooz a-play ?

how do you do!
bonjour
bON-zhoor

pleased to meet you!
enchanté !
ON-shON-tay !

this is my husband
je vous présente mon mari
zhuh voo pray-zONt mON ma-ree

this is my partner, Karen
je vous présente Karen, ma copine
zhuh voo pray-zONt Karen, ma koh-peen

I'm English
je suis anglais(e)
zhuh sweez ON-glay(z)

we're Welsh
nous sommes gallois
noo som gal-wa

I'm from …
je viens de …
zhuh vyAN duh …

where are you from?
vous êtes d'où ?
vooz et doo ?

how old are you?
quel âge as-tu ?
kel azh a tU ?

I'm 22
j'ai 22 ans
zhay vANt-duhz ON

what do you do for a living?
qu'est-ce vous faites dans la vie ?
kess-kuh voo fet dON la vee ?

are you a student?
tu es étudiant ?
tU ay ay-tU-dyON ?

I work
je travaille
zhuh tra-va-y

I'm studying law
je fais des études de droit
zhuh fay dayz ay-tUd duh drwa

I'm a teacher
je suis prof
zhuh swee prof

I stay at home with the children
je ne travaille pas, je m'occupe des enfants
zhu nuh tra-va-y pa, zhuh mo-kUp dayz ON-fON

I work part-time
je travaille à temps partiel
zhuh tra-va-y a tON pars-yel

I work in marketing
je travaille dans le marketing
zhuh tra-va-y dON luh mar-ke-teeng

I'm retired
je suis à la retraite
zhuh sweez a la ruh-tret

I'm self-employed
je travaille à mon compte
zhuh tra-va-y a mON kONt

I have two children
j'ai deux enfants
zhay duhz ON-fON

we don't have any children
nous n'avons pas d'enfants
noo navON pa dON-fON

two boys and a girl
deux garçons et une fille
duh gar-sON ay Un fee

a boy of five and a girl of two
un garçon de cinq ans et une fille de deux ans
AN gar-sON duh sANk ON ay Un fee duh duhz ON

have you ever been to Britain?
est-ce que vous êtes déjà allé en Grande-Bretagne ?
ess-kuh vooz et day-zha alay ON grONd-bruh-tan-yuh ?

Understanding

vous êtes anglais ?
are you English?

je connais assez bien l'Angleterre
I know England quite well

nous aussi, on est en vacances ici
we're on holiday here too

j'aimerais beaucoup aller en Écosse un jour
I'd love to go to Scotland one day

TALKING ABOUT YOUR STAY

Expressing yourself

we're on holiday
nous sommes en vacances
noo somz ON va-kONs

I'm here on business
je suis ici pour mon travail
zhuh sweez ee-see poor mON tra-va-y

we've been here for a week
ça fait une semaine qu'on est ici
sa fay Un suh-men kON ayt ee-see

I arrived three days ago
je suis arrivé il y a trois jours
zhuh sweez a-ree-vay eel ya trwa zhoor

I'm only here for a long weekend
je ne suis ici que pour un long week-end
zhuh nuh sweez ee-see kuh poor AN lON wee-kend

we're just passing through
on est seulement de passage
ON ay suhl-mON duh pa-sazh

we're on our honeymoon
c'est notre voyage de noces
say not-ruh vwa-yazh duh nos

this is our first time in France
c'est la première fois que nous venons en France
say la pruhm-yer fwa kuh noo vuh-nON ON frONs

we're here to celebrate our wedding anniversary
nous sommes ici pour notre anniversaire de mariage
noo somz ee-see poor notr a-nee-ver-ser duh mar-yazh

we're here with friends
on est ici avec des amis
ON ayt ee-see avek dayz amee

we're touring around
on visite la région
ON vee-zeet la rayzh-yON

we managed to get a cheap flight
on a trouvé un vol pas cher
ON a troo-vay AN vol pa sher

we're thinking about buying a house here
nous pensons à acheter une maison ici
noo pON-sONz a ash-tay Un may-zON ee-see

Understanding

bonnes vacances !
have a good holiday!

bon séjour !
enjoy your stay!

bonne fin de vacances !
enjoy the rest of your holiday!

à la prochaine !
see you!

c'est la première fois que vous venez dans la vallée de la Loire ?
is this your first time in the Loire Valley?

vous êtes ici pour combien de temps ?
how long are you staying?

ça te/vous plaît (ici) ?
do you like it here?

est-ce que vous avez été à … ?
have you been to …?

STAYING IN TOUCH

Expressing yourself

we should stay in touch
on reste en contact, hein ?
ON rest ON kON-takt, AN ?

I'll give you my e-mail address
je vais vous donner mon adresse e-mail
zhuh vay voo doh-nay mONn a-dres ee-mayl

here's my address, if ever you come to Britain
voilà mon adresse, si vous venez un jour en Grande-Bretagne
vwa-la mONn a-dres, see voo vuh-nay AN zhoor ON grONd-bruh-tan-yuh

Understanding

tu me donnes ton adresse ?
will you give me your address?

est-ce que vous avez une adresse e-mail ?
do you have an e-mail address?

vous êtes toujours les bienvenus chez nous
you're always welcome to come and stay with us here

EXPRESSING YOUR OPINION

> **Some informal expressions**
> **c'était nul** it was a complete waste of time
> **c'était chiant** it was deadly boring
> **on s'est bien éclatés** we had a fantastic time

Expressing yourself

I really like …
j'aime beaucoup …
zhem boh-koo …

I really liked …
j'ai vraiment aimé …
zhay vray-mON ay-may …

I don't like …
je n'aime pas …
zhuh nem pa …

I didn't like …
je n'ai pas aimé …
zhuh nay paz ay-may …

I love …
j'adore …
zha-dor …

I loved …
j'ai adoré …
zhay a-doh-ray …

I would like …
j'aimerais …
zhe-muh-ray …

I would have liked …
j'aurais aimé …
zhoh-ray ay-may …

I find it …
je trouve ça …
zhuh troov sa …

I found it …
j'ai trouvé ça …
zhay troo-vay sa …

it's lovely
c'est magnifique
say ma-nee-feek

it was lovely
c'était magnifique
say-tay ma-nee-feek

I agree
je suis d'accord
zhuh swee da-kor

I don't agree
je ne suis pas d'accord
zhuh nuh swee pa da-kor

I don't know
je ne sais pas
zhuh nuh say pa

I don't mind
ça m'est égal
sa met ay-gal

GETTING TO
KNOW PEOPLE

19

I don't like the sound of it
ça ne me dit rien
sa nuh muh dee ree-AN

it really annoys me
ça m'énerve vraiment
sa may-nerv vray-mON

it's a rip-off
c'est de l'arnaque
say duh lar-nak

it's too busy
il y a trop de monde
eel ya troh duh mONd

I really enjoyed myself
je me suis bien amusé
zhuh muh swee byAN a-mU-zay

there was a really good atmosphere
il y avait une ambiance très sympa
eel ya-vay Un ON-byONs tray sAN-pa

we found a great hotel
on a trouvé un hôtel très bien
ON a troo-vay AN oh-tel tray byAN

it sounds interesting
ça a l'air intéressant
sa a ler AN-tay-re-sON

it was boring
c'était ennuyeux
say-tay ON-nwee-yuh

it gets very busy at night
c'est très animé le soir
say trayz a-nee-may luh swar

it's very quiet
il n'y a pas grand monde
eel nya pa grON mONd

we had a great time
c'était super
say-tay sU-per

we met some nice people
on a rencontré des gens sympas
ON a rON-kON-tray day zhON sAN-pa

GETTING TO
KNOW PEOPLE

Understanding

est-ce que tu aimes/vous aimez … ?
do you like …?

vous avez passé du bon temps ?
did you enjoy yourselves?

je vous recommande …
I recommend …

c'est une très belle région
it's a lovely area

vous devriez aller à …
you should go to …

ce n'est pas trop touristique
there aren't too many tourists

n'y allez pas le week-end, il y a trop de monde
don't go at the weekend, it's too busy

TALKING ABOUT THE WEATHER

Some informal expressions

il faisait un froid de canard it was freezing cold
il faisait une chaleur à crever it was scorching
il tombait des cordes it was pouring with rain

Expressing yourself

have you seen the weather forecast for tomorrow?
est-ce que vous avez vu la météo pour demain ?
ess-kuh vooz avay vU la may-tay-oh poor duh-mAN ?

it's going to be nice
il va faire beau
eel va fer boh

it isn't going to be nice
il ne va pas faire beau
eel nuh va pa fer boh

it's really hot
il fait vraiment chaud
eel fay vray-mON shoh

it gets cold at night
il fait froid la nuit
eel fay frwa la nwee

the weather was beautiful
il a fait un temps superbe
eel a fay AN tON sU-perb

it rained a few times
il a plu quelques fois
eel a plU kel-kuh fwa

there was a thunderstorm
il y a eu un orage
eel ya U AN oh-razh

it's been lovely all week
il a fait beau toute la semaine
eel a fay boh toot la suh-men

we've been lucky with the weather
on a eu de la chance avec le temps
ON a U duh la shONs avek luh tON

Understanding

il paraît qu'il va pleuvoir
it's supposed to rain

il va encore faire chaud demain
it's going to be hot again tomorrow

ils ont prévu du beau temps pour le reste de la semaine
they've forecast good weather for the rest of the week

GETTING TO
KNOW PEOPLE

21

TRAVELLING

The basics

airport	aéroport *ah-ay-roh-por*
boarding	embarquement *ON-bar-kuh-mON*
boarding card	carte d'embarquement *kart dON-bar-kuh-mON*
boat	bateau *ba-toh*
bus	bus *bUs*
bus station	gare routière *gar roo-tyer*
bus stop	arrêt de bus *a-ray duh bUs*
car	voiture *vwa-tUr*
check-in	enregistrement *ON-ruh-zhees-truh-mON*
coach	autocar *oh-toh-kar*, **car** *kar*
coach station	gare routière *gar roo-tyer*
ferry	ferry *fay-ree*
flight	vol *vol*
gate	porte (d'embarquement) *port (dON-bar-kuh-mON)*
left-luggage (office)	(bureau des) objets trouvés *(bU-roh dayz) ob-zhay troo-vay*
luggage	bagages *ba-gazh*
map	carte *kart*
motorway	autoroute *oh-toh-root*
passport	passeport *pas-por*
plane	avion *av-yON*
platform	quai *kay*
railway station	gare *gar*
return (ticket)	aller-retour *alay-ruh-toor*
road	route *root*; (street) rue *rU*
shuttle bus	navette *na-vet*
single (ticket)	aller (simple) *alay (sANpl)*
street	rue *rU*
streetmap	plan (de la ville) *plAN (duh la veel)*
taxi	taxi *tak-see*
terminal	terminal *ter-mee-nal*
ticket	*(for bus, underground)* ticket *tee-kay*, *(for train, plane)* billet *bee-yay*

timetable	horaires *o-rer*
town centre	**centre-ville** *sON-truh-veel*
train	**train** *trAN*
tram	**tramway** *tramway*
underground	**métro** *may-troh*
underground station	**station de métro** *stass-yON duh may-troh*
to book	**réserver** *ray-zer-vay*
to hire	**louer** *loo-ay*

Expressing yourself

where can I buy tickets?
où est-ce que je peux acheter des billets ?
oo ess-kuh zhuh puh ash-tay day bee-yay ?

a ticket to …, please
un billet pour …
AN bee-yay poor …

I'd like to book a ticket
je voudrais réserver un billet
zhuh voo-dray ray-zer-vay AN bee-yay

how much is a ticket to …?
combien coûte un billet pour … ?
kom-byAN koot AN bee-yay poor … ?

are there any concessions for students?
est-ce qu'il y a des réductions pour les étudiants ?
ess keel ya day ray-dUk-syON poor layz ay-tU-dyAN ?

could I have a timetable, please?
est-ce que je peux avoir un dépliant avec les horaires ?
ess kuh zhuh puh av-war AN day-plee-yAN avek layz o-rer ?

is there an earlier/later one?
y en a-t-il un plus tôt/tard ?
yON-a-teel AN plU toh/tar ?

how long does the journey take?
combien de temps dure le voyage ?
kom-byAN duh tON dUr luh vwa-yazh ?

is this seat free?
est-ce que cette place est libre ?
ess kuh set plass ay leebr ?

I'm sorry, there's someone sitting there
désolé, il y a déjà quelqu'un
day-zoh-lay, eel ya day-zha kel-kAN

Understanding

Making sense of abbreviations

A/R (= aller-retour) return (ticket)
Arr (= arrivée) arrival
Dép (= départ) departure
PC (= petite ceinture) Paris inner ring road
RER (= réseau express régional) express train network in the Paris region
SNCF (= Société nationale des chemins de fer français) French national rail company
TER (= train express régional) regional express train
TGV (= train à grande vitesse) high speed train

Days of the week: **lun**, **mar**, **mer**, **jeu**, **ven**, **sam**, **dim**, or **lu**, **ma**, **me**, **je**, **ve**, **sa**, **di**.
On timetables, **tlj** stands for **tous les jours** (every day), and **sf dim** for **sauf le dimanche** (except Sundays).

accueil	information
annulé	cancelled
arrivées	arrivals
billeterie	tickets
billeterie automatique	ticket machine
correspondances	connections
départs	departures
entrée	entrance
renseignements	information
retardé	delayed
sortie	exit
toilettes	toilets

il ne reste plus de places
there are no seats left

tout est complet
everything is fully booked

BY PLANE

Expressing yourself

where's the British Airways check-in?
où est l'enregistrement des bagages pour British Airways ?
oo ay lON-ruh-zhees-truh-mON day ba-gazh poor British Airways ?

I've got an e-ticket
j'ai acheté mon billet sur Internet
zhay ash-tay mON bee-yay sUr AN-ter-net

one suitcase and one piece of hand luggage
une valise et un bagage à main
Un va-leez ay AN ba-gazh a mAN

what time do we board?
à quelle heure embarque-t-on ?
a kel uhr ON-bar-kuh-tON ?

I'd like to confirm my return flight
je voudrais confirmer mon vol de retour
zhuh voo-dray kON-feer-may mON vol duh ruh-toor

one of my suitcases is missing
il me manque une valise
eel muh mONk Un va-leez

my luggage hasn't arrived
mes bagages ne sont pas arrivés
may ba-gazh nuh sON paz a-ree-vay

I've missed my connection
j'ai raté ma correspondance
zhay ra-tay ma ko-res-pON-dONs

the plane was two hours late
l'avion a eu deux heures de retard
lav-yON a U duhz uhr duh ruh-tar

I've left something on the plane
j'ai oublié quelque chose dans l'avion
zhay oo-blee-yay kel-kuh-shohz dAN lav-yON

I want to report the loss of my luggage
je voudrais faire une déclaration de perte pour mes bagages
zhuh voo-dray fer Un day-kla-ra-syON duh pert poor may ba-gazh

Understanding

contrôle des passeports	passport control
douane	customs

embarquement immédiat	immediate boarding
enregistrement	check-in
marchandises à déclarer	goods to declare
ressortissants de l'UE	EU passport holders
retrait des bagages	baggage reclaim
rien à déclarer	nothing to declare
salle d'embarquement	departure lounge
vols intérieurs	domestic flights

veuillez patienter dans la salle d'embarquement
please wait in the departure lounge

voulez-vous une place côté hublot ou côté couloir ?
would you like a window seat or an aisle seat?

vous avez une correspondance à …
you'll have to change in …

combien de bagages avez-vous ?
how many bags do you have?

avez-vous fait vous-même tous vos bagages ?
did you pack all your bags yourself?

quelqu'un vous a-t-il donné quelque chose à emporter à bord ?
has anyone given you anything to take on board?

vous avez un excédent de cinq kilos
your luggage is five kilos overweight

voilà votre carte d'embarquement
here's your boarding card

l'embarquement commencera à …
boarding will begin at …

veuillez vous rendre à la porte numéro …
please proceed to gate number …

dernier appel pour …
this is a final call for …

vous pouvez appeler ce numéro pour savoir si vos bagages sont arrivés
you can call this number to check that your luggage has arrived

BY TRAIN, COACH, BUS, UNDERGROUND, TRAM

Tickets for all forms of public transport except buses need to be bought in advance. For high-speed trains (**TGV**) the ticket includes a seat reservation. The number of the coach (**voiture**) and the seat number (**place assise**) are marked on the ticket. For all trains you need to punch your ticket in one of the orange machines before going onto the platform. You should always note the number of the train. This is printed on the ticket eg TGV 9833. This is important since when you look at the indicator board in the station, it will only give the final destination of the train and not the stations it will stop at en route.

When you get on a bus or tram, there is a machine for you to punch your ticket. It is an offence not to do so.

When using the underground, you need to identify the end of the line for the line and direction you are going in. Indications such as northbound/southbound are not used.

Expressing yourself

can I have a map of the underground, please?
est-ce que je pourrais avoir un plan du métro ?
ess kuh zhuh poo-ray av-war AN plON dU may-troh ?

what time is the next train to ...?
à quelle heure est le prochain train pour ... ?
a kel uhr ay luh pro-shAN trAN poor ... ?

what time is the last train?
à quelle heure part le dernier train ?
a kel uhr par luh der-nyay trAN ?

which platform is it for the ... train?
de quel quai part le train pour ... ?
duh kel kay par luh trAN poor ... ?

where can I catch a bus to …?
où est-ce que je peux prendre un bus pour … ?
oo ess kuh juh puh prONdr AN bUs poor … ?

is this the stop for …?
c'est bien l'arrêt pour … ?
say byAN la-ray poor … ?

which line do I take to get to …?
quelle ligne dois-je prendre pour … ?
kel leen-yuh dwazh prONdr poor … ?

is this where the coach leaves for …?
c'est bien d'ici que part le car pour … ?
say byAN dee-see kuh par luh kar poor … ?

can you tell me when I need to get off?
pourriez-vous me dire quand je dois descendre ?
poor-yay voo muh deer kON zhuh dwa day-sONdr ?

Understanding

accès aux quais	to the trains
banlieue	to suburban trains
carte orange	travel pass
départs dans la journée	tickets for travel today
grandes lignes	to main-line trains
hebdomadaire	weekly
mensuel	monthly
réservations	bookings

côté fenêtre ou côté couloir ?
a window seat or an aisle seat?

vous avez un changement à …
you'll have to change at …

il y a un arrêt un peu plus loin à droite
there's a stop a bit further along on the right

vous devez prendre le bus numéro …
you need to get the number … bus

allez jusqu'au terminus
go to the terminus

ce train dessert les gares de …
this train calls at …

le train en provenance de …
the train arriving from …

le train à destination de …
the train for …

le prochain arrêt est …
the next stop is …

BY CAR

France has an excellent road network with many toll motorways (**autoroutes**, signposted in blue and numbered A6, A7 etc) and dual carriageways (**routes à quatres voies**, signposted in red). The trunk roads (**routes nationales**), signposted in green and numbered ((R)N6, (R)N7 etc) are also good. It is always possible to take one of these instead of a toll motorway and many offer more scenic routes. Speed limits are 130 km/h on motorways and 120 km/h on dual carriageways. Unless otherwise stated, the speed limit in towns and villages is 50 km/h. There are regular stopping places (**aires**) on motorways. Signs indicate the facilities offered. At tollgates (**péages**) you can pay by card using an automatic machine at gates indicated **CB** (**carte bancaire**) and by card or cash at the staffed gates indicated with a green arrow. Note that French law obliges drivers to carry photo identity, driving licence, car registration papers and insurance details at all times. As in Britain, seatbelts are obligatory in both front and rear seats and the legal alcohol limit is just a little over half of what it is in Britain.

Taxi drivers will usually ask you to pay extra for luggage. Tipping is discretionary.

Expressing yourself

where can I find a petrol station?
où est-ce que je peux trouver une station-service ?
oo ess kuh zhuh puh troo-vay Un stass-yON ser-vees ?

lead-free petrol, please
du sans-plomb, s'il vous plaît
dU sON plON, seel voo play

how much is it per litre?
c'est combien le litre ?
say kON-byAN luh leetr ?

we got stuck in a traffic jam
on a été bloqués dans un embouteillage
ON na ay-tay blo-kay dOnz AN ON-boo-tay-yazh

is there a garage near here?
y a-t-il un garagiste par ici ?
ya-teel AN ga-ra-zheest par ee-see ?

can you help us to push the car?
pourriez-vous nous aider à pousser la voiture ?
poor-yay voo nooz ay-day a poo-say la vwa-tUr ?

the battery's dead
la batterie est morte
la ba-tree ay mort

I've broken down
je suis tombé en panne
zhuh swee tON-bay ON pan

we've run out of petrol
on est en panne d'essence
ON nayt ON pan day-sONs

I've lost my car keys
j'ai perdu mes clés de voiture
zhay per-dU may klay duh vwa-tUr

I've got a puncture and my spare tyre is flat
j'ai crevé et la roue de secours est à plat
zhay kruh-vay ay la roo duh suh-koor ayt a pla

we've just had an accident
nous venons d'avoir un accident
noo vuh-nON da-vwar AN ak-si-dON

how long will it take to repair?
ça va prendre combien de temps à réparer ?
sa va prONdr kON-byAN duh tON a ray-pa-ray ?

◆ Hiring a car

I'd like to hire a car for a week
je voudrais louer une voiture pour une semaine
zhuh voo-dray loo-ay Un vwa-tUr poor Un suh-men

an automatic (car)
une voiture à boîte de vitesses automatique
Un vwa-tUr a bwat duh vee-tess oh-toh-ma-teek

we need a child seat
nous aurions besoin d'un siège-auto pour enfant
nooz oh-ryON buh-zwAN dAN syezh poor ON-fON

◆ Getting a taxi

is there a taxi rank near here?
y a-t-il une station de taxis près d'ici ?
ya-teel Un stass-yON duh tak-see pray dee-see ?

I'd like to go to …
je vais à …
zhuh vayz a …

I'd like to book a taxi for 8pm
je voudrais un taxi pour 20 heures
juh voo-dray AN tak-see poor vANt uhr

you can drop me off here, thanks
vous pouvez m'arrêter ici, merci
voo poo-vay ma-ray-tay ee-see, mer-see

how much will it be to go to the airport?
combien ça va me coûter pour aller à l'aéroport ?
kON-byAN sa va muh koo-tay poor alay a la-ay-roh-por ?

◆ Hitchhiking

I'm going to …
je vais à …
zhuh vayz a …

thanks for the lift
merci de m'avoir emmené
mer-see duh mav-war ON-mnay

can you drop me off here?
est-ce que vous pourriez m'arrêter ici ?
ess-kuh voo poor-yay ma-ray-tay ee-see ?

could you take me as far as …?
pourriez-vous m'emmener jusqu'à … ?
poor-yay voo mON-mnay zhUska … ?

we hitched a lift
on a fait du stop
ON na fay dU stop

Understanding

autres directions	other directions
bouchon	congestion ahead
complet	full *(car park)*
conservez votre ticket	keep your ticket with you

location de voitures	car hire
parking	car park
péage	tollgate
périphérique, périph	ring road
places libres	spaces *(car park)*
ralentissez	slow down
stationnement interdit	no parking
toutes directions	all directions

il me faut votre permis de conduire, une pièce d'identité, un justificatif de domicile et votre carte de paiement
I'll need your driving licence, another form of ID, proof of address and your credit card

il y a une caution de 150 euros
there's a 150 euro deposit

c'est bon, montez, je vais vous avancer jusqu'à …
OK, get in, I'll take you as far as …

BY BOAT

Expressing yourself

how long is the crossing?	**I'm seasick**
combien dure la traversée ?	j'ai le mal de mer
kON-byAN dUr la tra-ver-say ?	*jay luh mal duh mer*

Understanding

passagers sans véhicule	foot passengers only
prochain départ à …	next crossing at …
traversée toutes les heures	hourly crossings

Hotels (**hôtels**) in France are classified according to a star system, as in the UK – and priced accordingly. Those classified by Logis de France generally offer a good standard of accommodation and food at a reasonable price. They publish a guide annually. Prices are usually displayed outside hotels. You can also find **chambres d'hôtes** (bed and breakfast). Some of these offer a **table d'hôte** service, providing lunch and/or dinner.

If you are looking for self-catering accommodation, the organization Gîtes de France offers a wide variety from **résidences de tourisme** (luxury service apartments) to **camping à la ferme** (camping on a farm). In between, there are **gîtes ruraux** (country cottages) and **chalets-loisirs** (small chalets in rural areas). The classification system for gîtes uses an ear of corn symbol (**épis**). All accommodation registered with Gîtes de France has to conform to certain standards. A comprehensive guide to Gîtes de France is available at bookstores in both France and the UK. They also have a website.

There are good youth hostels (**auberges de jeunesse**, abbreviation **AJ**).

Campsites, both privately and municipally run, are generally excellent, with good facilities for small children. They are very reasonably priced.

If you have not booked in advance, the best bet is to head for the local tourist office (**Office de tourisme** or **Syndicat d'initiative**) where you will find all the information on accommodation options in the area.

Note that in order to use a British electrical appliance, you will need a continental adaptor, available in electrical shops in the UK.

The basics

air conditioning	climatisation *klee-ma-tee-zas-yON*
bath	baignoire *ben-war*
bathroom	salle de bains *sal duh bAN*

bathroom with shower	salle de bains avec douche *sal duh bAN avek doosh*
bed	lit *lee*
bed and breakfast	chambre d'hôtes *shON-bruh doht*
campsite	camping *kON-peeng*
caravan	caravane *ka-ra-van*
double bed	lit double *lee doobl*
double room	chambre double *shON-bruh doobl*
en-suite bathroom	chambre avec salle de bains *shONbr avek sal duh bAN*
family room	chambre familiale *shON-bruh fa-meel-yal*
flat	appartement *a-par-tuh-mON*
full-board	pension complète *pONs-yON kON-plet*
fully inclusive	tout compris *too kON-pree*
half-board	demi-pension *duh-mee-pONs-yON*
holiday cottage	gîte *zheet*
hotel	hôtel *oh-tel*
rent	loyer *lwa-yay*
satellite television	télévision par satellite *tay-lay-veez-yON par sa-tay-leet*
self-catering accommodation	location *loh-kas-yON*
shower	douche *doosh*
single bed	lit pour une personne *lee poor Un per-son*
single room	chambre individuelle/simple *shONbr AN-dee-vee-dU-el/sANpl*
tenant	locataire *loh-ka-ter*
tent	tente *tONt*
toilets	toilettes *twa-let*
youth hostel	auberge de jeunesse *oh-berzh duh zhuh-nes*
to book	réserver *ray-zer-vay*
to rent	louer *loo-ay*

Expressing yourself

I have a reservation
j'ai fait une réservation
zhay fay Un ray-zer-vas-yON

the name's ...
mon nom est ...
mON nON ay ...

34

do you take credit cards?
est-ce qu'on peut payer par carte ?
ess-kON puh pay-yay par kart ?

Understanding

accueil	reception
arrhes	deposit
chambres libres	vacancies
complet	full
privé	private
réception	reception
sdb (= **s**alle de bains)	bathroom
toilettes	toilets

HOTELS

Expressing yourself

do you have any vacancies?
est-ce qu'il vous reste une chambre de libre ?
ess keel voo rest Un shONbr duh leebr ?

how much is a double room per night?
combien coûte une chambre double ?
kON-byAN koot Un shON-bruh doobl ?

I'd like to book a double room/a single room
je voudrais réserver une chambre double/chambre individuelle
zhuh voo-dray ray-zer-vay Un shON-bruh doobl/shONbr AN-dee-vee-dU-el

for three nights
pour trois nuits
poor trwa nwee

would it be possible to stay an extra night?
serait-il possible de rester une nuit de plus ?
suh-ray-teel poh-seebl duh res-tay Un nwee duh plUs ?

do you have any rooms available for tonight?
est-ce qu'il vous reste une chambre de libre pour cette nuit ?
ess keel voo rest Un shONbr duh leebr poor set nwee ?

do you have any family rooms?
avez-vous des chambres familiales ?
avay-voo day shONbr fa-meel-yal ?

would it be possible to add an extra bed?
serait-il possible d'avoir un lit supplémentaire ?
suh-ray-teel poh-seebl dav-war AN lee sU-play-mON-ter ?

could I see the room first?
est-ce que je pourrais d'abord voir la chambre ?
ess-kuh zhuh poo-ray da-bor vwar la shONbr ?

do you have anything bigger/quieter?
avez-vous quelque chose de plus grand/calme ?
avay-voo kel-kuh-shohz duh plU grON/kalm ?

that's fine, I'll take it
c'est bon, je la prends
say bON, zhuh la prON

is there a lift?
y a-t-il un ascenseur ?
ya-teel AN a-sON-suhr ?

could you recommend any other hotels?
pourriez-vous me recommander d'autres hôtels ?
poor-yay-voo muh ruh-koh-mON-day doh-truhz ohtel ?

is breakfast included?
le petit déjeuner est-il compris ?
luh puh-tee day-zhuh-nay ay-teel kON-pree ?

what time do you serve breakfast?
à quelle heure est servi le petit déjeuner ?
a kel uhr ay ser-vee luh puh-tee day-zhuh-nay ?

is the hotel near the centre of town?
est-ce que l'hôtel est près du centre ?
ess-kuh lohtel ay pray dU sONtr ?

what time will the room be ready?
à quelle heure la chambre sera-t-elle prête ?
a kel uhr la shONbr suhra-tel pret ?

the key for room …, please
la clé de la chambre …, s'il vous plaît
la klay duh la shONbr …, seel voo play

could I have an extra blanket?
est-ce que je pourrais avoir une couverture en plus ?
ess-kuh zhuh poo-ray av-war Un koo-ver-tUr ON plUs ?

the air conditioning isn't working
la climatisation ne marche pas
la klee-ma-tee-zas-yON nuh marsh pa

Understanding

je regrette mais nous sommes complets
I'm sorry, but we're full

il ne nous reste qu'une chambre double
we only have a double room available

c'est pour combien de nuits ?   **à quel nom, s'il vous plaît ?**
how many nights is it for?   what's your name, please?

les chambres sont disponibles à partir de midi
check-in is from midday

la chambre doit être libérée avant midi
you have to check out before midday

le petit déjeuner est servi dans le restaurant entre 8 et 10h
breakfast is served in the restaurant between 8am and 10am

votre chambre n'est pas encore prête
your room isn't ready yet

vous pouvez laisser vos bagages ici
you can leave your bags here

YOUTH HOSTELS

Expressing yourself

do you have space for two people for tonight?
est-ce qu'il vous reste de la place pour deux personnes pour cette nuit ?
ess-keel voo rest duh la plas poor duh per-son poor set nwee ?

we've booked two beds for three nights
on a réservé pour deux personnes pour trois nuits
ON a ray-zer-vay poor duh per-son poor trwa nwee

could I leave my backpack at reception?
est-ce que je peux laisser mon sac à dos à la réception ?
ess-kuh zhuh puh lay-say mON sak a-doh a la ray-seps-yoN ?

do you have somewhere we could leave our bikes?
est-ce qu'il y a un endroit où on pourrait laisser nos vélos ?
ess-keel ya AN ON-drwa oo ON poo-ray lay-say noh vay-loh ?

I'll come back for it around 7 o'clock
je viendrais le chercher vers sept heures
zhuh vyAN-dray luh sher-shay ver set uhr

there's no hot water
il n'y a pas d'eau chaude
eel nya pa doh shohd

the sink's blocked
l'évier est bouché
lay-vyay ay blo-kay

Understanding

est-ce que vous avez une carte de membre ?
do you have a membership card?

les draps sont fournis
bed linen is provided

l'auberge rouvre à six heures
the hostel reopens at 6pm

SELF-CATERING

Expressing yourself

we're looking for somewhere to rent near a town
nous cherchons une location à proximité d'une ville
noo sher-shON Un loh-kas-yON a prok-see-mee-tay dUn veel

where do we pick up/leave the keys?
où doit-on prendre/laisser les clés ?
oo dwat-ON prONdr/lay-say lay klay ?

is electricity included in the price?
l'électricité est-elle comprise dans le prix ?
lay-lek-tree-see-tay ayt-el kON-preez dON luh pree ?

are bed linen and towels provided?
les draps et serviettes sont-ils fournis ?
lay dra ay serv-yet sON-teel foor-nee ?

is there a pool?
y a-t-il une piscine ?
ya-teel Un pee-seen ?

is a car necessary?
faut-il avoir une voiture ?
foh-teel av-war Un vwa-tUr ?

is the accommodation suitable for elderly people?
la location conviendrait-elle à des personnes âgées ?
la loh-kas-yON kON-vyAN-dret-el a day per-son za-zhay ?

where is the nearest supermarket?
où est le supermarché le plus proche ?
oo ay luh sU-per-mar-shay luh plU prosh ?

Understanding

veuillez laisser la maison dans l'état où vous l'avez trouvée
please leave the house clean and tidy when you leave

la maison est entièrement meublée
the house is fully furnished

tout est inclus dans le prix
everything is included in the price

il est indispensable d'avoir une voiture dans cette région
you really need a car in this part of the country

CAMPING

Expressing yourself

is there a campsite near here?
est-ce qu'il y a un camping par ici ?
ess-keel ya AN kON-peeng par ee-see ?

I'd like to book a space for a four-person tent for three nights
je voudrais réserver un emplacement pour une tente de quatre
personnes pour trois jours
*zhuh voo-dray ray-zer-vay AN ON-plas-mON poor Un tONt duh kat per-son
poor trwa zhoor*

how much is it a night?
ça coûte combien par jour ?
sa koot kON-byAN par zhoor ?

where is the shower block?
où sont les douches ?
oo sON lay doosh ?

can we pay, please? we were at space …
nous venons régler – nous étions à l'emplacement …
noo vuh-nON ray-glay – nooz ay-tyON a lON-plas-mON …

Understanding

c'est … par personne et par jour
it's … per person per night

n'hésitez pas à demander si vous avez besoin de quoique ce soit
if you need anything, just come and ask

EATING AND DRINKING

Everybody knows that when you go to France there is no problem about being able to eat well. Restaurants (**restaurants**), even in big cities, vary from the internationally renowned to small family-run establishments. **Brasseries** and **bistrots** are generally modest but can also be quite grand – and expensive. You will always find the menu displayed outside so you can check out what type of food is on offer and whether the prices suit your budget. In a modest brasserie or restaurant you will find a variety of simple starters, main courses and desserts along with the day's specials (**plats du jour**).

Wherever you are, the best-value option is often to choose a set menu (**menu**). If you opt for a three-course menu, you usually have the choice between cheese or dessert. Cheese is served before dessert. You can also choose from the **à la carte** menu where each dish is priced separately. In rural areas, look out for menus offering local specialities (**menu terroir**). A simple menu for children (**menu d'enfant**) is usually available.

In many cafés and most brasseries you can find quick snacks (**casse-croûte**), sandwiches and salads.

Lunch is still regarded as the important meal in many contexts in France. Service begins at midday. In most restaurants you will not be served after 2pm. In the evening, service will begin around 7pm. In rural areas, service will stop at around 9pm whilst the big brasseries in cities serve until late in the evening.

Pizza and hamburger restaurants can be found almost everywhere. France also offers a variety of ethnic food, especially North African, Vietnamese and Cambodian.

Wherever you eat, as much bread and tap water as you want is provided free of charge. In more modest restaurants, you can order a jug (**pichet**) of the house wine. You can choose the quantity. You will often be asked whether you want a pre-meal drink (**apéritif**). Popular choices are **Pernod** and **kir** (white wine flavoured with blackcurrant liqueur). Service is always included but a tip according to quality of service is expected.

Cafés are usually open from early in the morning until late at night (though they generally close fairly early in rural areas). Always sit down and wait for table service. Note that if you order a coffee (**un café**) this will always be a small expresso without milk. A coffee with milk is **un café crème**. Cafés usually serve a variety of alcoholic drinks, including both bottled and draught lager. To order the latter ask for **un demi** or **une pression** (a little less than a British half). The age limit for drinking alcohol is 18.

The basics

beer	bière *byer*
bill	addition *a-dees-yON*
black coffee	café *ka-fay*
bottle	bouteille *boo-tey*
bread	pain *pAN*
breakfast	petit déjeuner *puh-tee day-zhuh-nay*
coffee	café *ka-fay*
Coke®	coca *ko-ka*
dessert	dessert *day-ser*
dinner	dîner *dee-nay*
fruit juice	jus de fruit *zhU duh frwee*
lemonade	limonade *lee-moh-nad*
lunch	déjeuner *day-zhuh-nay*
main course	plat (principal) *pla (prAN-see-pal)*
menu	carte *kart*
mineral water	eau minérale *oh mee-nay-ral*
red wine	vin rouge *vAN roozh*
rosé wine	rosé *roh-zay*
salad	salade *sa-lad*
sandwich	sandwich *sON-dweech*
service	service *ser-vees*
sparkling water	eau gazeuse *oh ga-zuhz*
starter	entrée *ON-tray*
still water	eau plate *oh plat*
tea	thé *tay*

tip	pourboire *poor-bwar*
water	eau *oh*
white coffee	café crème *ka-fay krem*
white wine	vin blanc *vAN blON*
wine	vin *vAN*
wine list	liste des vins *leest day vAN*
to eat	manger *mON-zhay*
to have breakfast	prendre le petit déjeuner *prONdr luh puh-tee day-zhuh-nay*
to have dinner	dîner *dee-nay*
to have lunch	déjeuner *day-zhuh-nay*
to order	commander *koh-mON-day*

Expressing yourself

shall we go and have something to eat?
on va manger un bout ?
ON va mON-zhay AN boo ?

do you want to go for a drink?
ça te dit d'aller boire un verre ?
sa tuh dee dalay bwar AN ver ?

can you recommend a good restaurant?
est-ce vous pouvez me recommander un bon restaurant ?
ess-kuh voo poo-vay muh ruh-koh-mON-day AN bON res-toh-rON ?

I'm not very hungry
je n'ai pas très faim
zhuh nay pa tray fAN

excuse me! *(to call the waiter)*
s'il vous plaît !
seel voo play !

cheers!
tchin-tchin !
cheen-cheen !

that was lovely
c'était très bien
say-tay tray byAN

could you bring us an ashtray, please?
s'il vous plaît, est-ce qu'on pourrait avoir un cendrier ?
seel voo play, ess-kON poo-ray avvar AN sON-dree-ay ?

where are the toilets, please?
excusez-moi, où sont les toilettes ?
ek-skU-zay mwa, oo sON lay twa-let ?

Understanding

à emporter	takeaway
casse-croûte	snack
maison	home-made
menu	set menu
plat du jour	today's special
spécialités de la maison	our specialities
sur place	eating in

RESERVING A TABLE

Expressing yourself

I'd like to reserve a table for tomorrow evening
je voudrais réserver une table pour demain soir
zhuh voo-dray ray-zer-vay Un tabl poor duh-mAN swar

for two people
pour deux
poor duh

around 8 o'clock
vers huit heures
ver weet uhr

do you have a table available any earlier than that?
est-ce que vous avez une table de libre plus tôt ?
ess-kuh vooz avay Un tabl duh leebr plU toh ?

I've reserved a table – the name's ...
j'ai réservé au nom de ...
zhay ray-zer-vay oh nON duh ...

Understanding

réservé
reserved

pour quelle heure ?
for what time?

pour combien de personnes ?
for how many people?

c'est à quel nom ?
what's the name?

vous avez réservé ?
do you have a reservation?

cette table dans le coin vous convient ?
is that table in the corner OK for you?

je regrette mais nous sommes complet
I'm afraid we're full at the moment

ORDERING FOOD

Expressing yourself

yes, we're ready to order
oui, on a choisi
wee, ON a shwa-zee

I'll have that
je vais prendre ça
zhuh vay prONdr sa

no, could you give us a few more minutes?
non, donnez-nous encore un petit moment
nON, do-nay noo ON-kor AN puh-tee moh-mON

could I have …?
est-ce que je pourrais avoir … ?
ess-kuh zhuh poo-ray av-war … ?

I'd like …
je voudrais …
zhuh voo-dray …

I'm not sure, what's "sole meunière"?
je ne suis pas sûr, qu'est-ce que c'est "sole meunière" ?
zhuh nuh swee pa sUr, kess-kuh say sol muh-nyer ?

does it come with vegetables?
est-ce que c'est servi avec des légumes ?
ess-kuh say ser-vee avek day lay-gUm ?

what are today's specials?
quels sont les plats du jour ?
kel sON lay pla dU zhoor ?

and a bottle of red/white wine
et une bouteille de vin rouge/blanc
ay Un boo-tey duh vAN roozh/blON

what desserts do you have?
qu'est-ce que vous avez comme desserts ?
kess-kuh vooz avay kom day-ser ?

that's for me
c'est pour moi
say poor mwa

could we have some water, please
une carafe d'eau, s'il vous plaît
Un ka-raf doh seel voo play

this isn't what I ordered, I wanted …
ce n'est pas ce que j'ai commandé, j'avais demandé …
suh nay pa suh kuh zhay koh-mON-day, zhavay duh-mON-day …

could we have some more bread, please?
est-ce qu'on pourrait avoir un peu plus de pain, s'il vous plaît ?
ess-kON poo-ray av-war AN puh plUs duh pAN, seel voo play ?

could you bring us another jug of water, please?
est-ce que vous pourriez nous apporter une autre carafe d'eau, s'il vous
 plaît ?
ess-kuh voo poor-yay nooz a-por-tay Un oh-truh ka-raf doh, seel voo play ?

Understanding

fromage ou dessert au choix   choice of cheese or dessert

vous avez choisi ?
are you ready to order?

je vous laisse choisir et je reviens
I'll leave you to choose and I'll come back in a minute

désolé, il ne reste plus de …
I'm sorry, we don't have any … left

vous le voulez avec des frites ou de la salade ?
would you like that with chips or salad?

qu'est-ce que vous voulez boire ?
what would you like to drink?

est-ce que vous voulez un dessert ? un café ?
would you like dessert or coffee?

ça a été ?
was everything OK?

EATING AND DRINKING

46

BARS AND CAFÉS

Expressing yourself

I'd like...
je voudrais …
zhuh voo-dray …

a Coke®
un Coca®
AN koka

a diet Coke®
un Coca® light
AN koka la-eet

a glass of red/white wine
un verre de vin rouge/blanc
AN ver duh vAN roozh/blON

a black/white coffee
un café/café crème
AN ka-fay/ka-fay krem

a cup of tea
un thé
AN tay

a coffee and a croissant
un café et un croissant
AN ka-fay ay AN krwa-sON

a cup of hot chocolate
un chocolat chaud
AN shoh-koh-la shoh

the same again, please
la même chose, s'il vous plaît
la mem shohz, seel voo play

Some informal expressions

j'ai un petit creux I'm a bit peckish
je crève de faim I'm starving
bouffe food
bouffer to eat
picoler to booze
prendre une cuite to get plastered
avoir la gueule de bois to have a hangover

EATING AND DRINKING

47

Understanding

sans alcool
non-alcoholic

c'est un espace non-fumeur
this is a non-smoking area

qu'est-ce que vous prendrez ?
what would you like?

je vais devoir encaisser, s'il vous plaît
could I ask you to pay now, please?

THE BILL

Expressing yourself

the bill, please
l'addition s'il vous plaît
la-dees-yON seel voo play

how much do I owe you?
je vous dois combien ?
zhuh voo dwa kON-byAN ?

do you take credit cards?
est-ce qu'on peut payer par carte ?
ess-kON puh pay-yay par kart ?

I think there's a mistake in the bill
je crois qu'il y a une erreur dans l'addition
zhuh krwa keel ya Un e-ruhr dON la-dees-yON

is service included?
le service est-il compris ?
luh ser-vees ay-teel kON-pree ?

Understanding

vous réglez tout ensemble ?
are you all paying together?

oui, le service est compris
yes, service is included

FOOD AND DRINK

Understanding

à l'étouffée	braised
à point	medium rare
bien cuit	well done
bouilli	boiled
braisé	braised
cru	raw; *(milk)* unpasteurized
cuit au feu de bois	cooked in a wood-fired oven
doré	lightly browned
en morceaux	chopped
en tranches	sliced
faire bouillir	to boil
faire chauffer	to heat
faire gratiner	to brown (under the grill or in the oven)
farci	stuffed
fondu	melted
frit	fried
fumé	smoked
grillé	grilled
pané	breaded
poché	poached
poêlé	pan-fried
râpé	grated
rôti	roast
saignant	rare
salé	salted
sauté	sautéed
séché	dried
vapeur, à la vapeur	steamed

◆ **petits déjeuners, goûters** breakfasts, snacks

beurre	butter
biscotte	piece of toasted bread (often sold in packets)
brioche	brioche, bun

café	coffee
café au lait	white coffee
café crème	white coffee
chausson aux pommes	apple turnover
chocolat chaud	hot chocolate
confiture	jam
croissant (au beurre)	croissant (made with pure butter)
gelée de myrtilles	bilberry jelly
jus de fruit	fruit juice
madeleine	small sponge cake
miel	honey
pain	bread
pain au chocolat	chocolate-filled pastry
pain au lait	milk roll
pain aux raisins	raisin and custard pastry
pain perdu	French toast
quatre-quarts	rich sponge cake
tartine	piece of bread and butter
tartine grillée	piece of toast
thé	tea

◆ sur le pouce snacks

croque-madame	toasted ham and cheese sandwich topped with a fried egg
croque-monsieur	toasted ham and cheese sandwich
omelette (nature)	(plain) omelette

◆ apéritifs, amuse-gueule cocktail snacks and nibbles

bouchées à la reine	vol-au-vent
cacahouètes	peanuts
chips	crisps
feuilletés	puff pastry nibbles
œufs de caille	quails' eggs
olives	olives
petits gâteaux salés	savoury biscuits
saucisson	French salami
toasts	small pieces of bread with a savoury topping

A typical French lunch or dinner consists of a starter (**entrée**), a main course (**plat principal**), cheese (**fromage**) and dessert (**dessert**). At home families traditionally ate a big lunch and had a lighter meal or snack in the evening but this now varies greatly according to ways of life. Sunday lunch is often a big occasion when people invite friends or family for a lengthy, lavish meal.

◆ entrées starters

assiette de charcuterie	mixed platter of salami, ham, pâté etc
assiette de crudités	platter of assorted salads
bisque de homard	lobster bisque
carottes râpées	grated carrot salad
crème de champignons	mushroom soup
cuisses de grenouille	frogs' legs
escargots à la bourguignonne	snails stuffed with garlic butter
foie gras	foie gras (goose or duck liver, often as a pâté)
gâteau de foie de volaille	chicken-liver soufflé
œufs durs farcis	stuffed eggs
pâté de campagne	coarsely textured pork-based pâté
poireaux à la vinaigrette	leeks with vinaigrette dressing
rillettes de canard/porc	potted duck/pork
salade composée	mixed salad
salade de gésiers de canard confits	green salad with duck gizzards
salade de lentilles	lentil salad
salade de magret de canard	smoked duck breast salad
salade lyonnaise	green salad with bacon pieces, poached egg and croûtons
salade niçoise	mixed salad with tuna and anchovies
soufflé au fromage	cheese soufflé
soupe au pistou	Mediterranean vegetable soup flavoured with pesto

soupe à l'oignon	French onion soup
soupe de poisson	fish soup
taboulé	tabbouleh (couscous salad with tomato, lemon, herbs and olive oil)
terrine de lapin/poisson	rabbit/fish terrine
velouté d'asperges	cream of asparagus
velouté de volaille	chicken soup

◆ poissons et fruits de mer fish and shellfish

darne de saumon	salmon steak
daurade au four	oven-roasted sea bream
homard à l'américaine	lobster cooked with white wine, brandy, and tomatoes
moules à la vapeur	steamed mussels
moules marinières	mussels cooked with shallots and white wine
plateau de fruits de mer	seafood platter
sardines grillées	grilled sardines
sole meunière	Dover sole pan-fried in butter

◆ volaille poultry

canard à l'orange	duck with orange sauce
confit de canard/d'oie	preserved duck/goose
coq au vin	cockerel cooked in red wine
foie gras poêlé	pan-fried fresh foie gras
fricassée de poulet	chicken with mushrooms in a cream sauce
pintade aux choux	guinea fowl with cabbage
poule au pot	boiling fowl poached with a variety of vegetables (the cooking liquid is usually served first as a soup)
poule au riz	boiling fowl poached with rice
poulet à l'estragon	tarragon chicken
poulet basquaise	chicken sautéed with tomatoes and green peppers

◆ gibier game

civet de lièvre	hare cooked with the blood and red wine and/or port
lapin à la moutarde	rabbit cooked in mustard and white wine
magret de canard	duck breast
poulet rôti	roast chicken
rôti de dinde	roast turkey
rôti de chevreuil	roast venison

◆ viandes meat

blanquette de veau	veal in a creamy sauce
bœuf bourguignon	rich, winey beef stew
bœuf en daube	beef marinated and cooked slowly in red wine
boudin aux pommes	black pudding with baked or fried apples
côtes/côtelettes d'agneau	lamb chops
côte de porc/veau	pork/veal chop
escalope de veau panée	breaded veal escalope
foie de veau en persillade	pan-fried veal liver with parsley and garlic
gigot d'agneau (au four)	roast leg of lamb
navarin d'agneau	lamb sautéed with spring vegetables
pavé de bœuf	thick steak
ris de veau	veal sweetbreads
rôti de porc aux pruneaux	roast pork stuffed with prunes
rôti de veau	roast veal
steak au poivre	pepper steak
steak tartare	steak tartare (raw, finely minced steak with seasoning)
tripes à la mode de Caen	tripe cooked in cider and Calvados

◆ accompagnements accompaniments

épinards à la crème	spinach with cream
gratin dauphinois	sliced potatoes baked in cream
gratin de macaronis	macaroni cheese

jardinière de légumes	mixed vegetables
pommes boulangères	potatoes cooked under a roast
pommes dauphine	lightly battered potato balls
pommes rissolées	sautéed cubed potatoes
ratatouille	stew of aubergines, peppers, courgettes and tomatoes
riz basquaise	rice pilaf with tomatoes and green peppers

◆ plats uniques composite dishes

bouillabaisse	Mediterranean fish stew
cassoulet	casserole of preserved goose, Toulouse sausage and white beans
choucroute garnie	pickled cabbage with various sausages, salt pork etc
endives au jambon	chicory wrapped in ham and baked in a creamy sauce
fondue bourguignonne	fondue consisting of a pan of hot oil in which you cook your own cubes of meat and select from a variety of sauces
fondue savoyarde	cheese fondue
hachis Parmentier	shepherd's pie
moules-frites	steamed mussels with French fries
petit salé aux lentilles	salt bacon cooked with lentils, carrots and onions
pot-au-feu	meat boiled with a variety of vegetables
raclette	dish consisting of cheese melted on a grill at the table and served with steamed potatoes and cured ham

♦ **fromage** cheese

France boasts an immense variety of cheeses of every type imaginable. Most regions have their own specialities and it is worth seeking these out in markets and in restaurants. In restaurants you are sometimes given the choice between fromage frais (**fromage blanc** in France) and a selection of cheeses. Cheese is always eaten before dessert.

♦ **desserts et pâtisseries** desserts and pastries

baba au rhum	rum baba
bavarois	creamy mousse, often containing fruit
beignets	fritters
bûche de Noël	chocolate Yule log
charlotte aux fruits rouges	red fruit mousse sourrounded by sponge fingers
clafoutis	fruit baked in a sweet batter
compote de pommes	apple puree
crêpe Suzette	crêpes flambéed in Cointreau
far breton	rich Breton prune cake
flan	custard tart
galette des Rois	puff-pastry cake filled with almond paste, traditionally eaten at Epiphany (6 January). It comes with a cardboard crown to be worn by the person who finds the little figure in the cake (la fève, so called because originally a bean was used)
gâteau de riz	caramelized rice pudding
gaufre	waffle
glace	ice cream
île flottante	whipped egg-white poached in vanilla custard
macédoine/salade de fruits	fruit salad
mille-feuille	puff pastry layered with vanilla custard
mousse au chocolat	chocolate mousse

poire Belle-Hélène	pears with ice cream and hot chocolate sauce
pomme au four	baked apple
tarte au citron	lemon tart
tarte aux noix/framboises	walnut/raspberry tart
tarte Tatin	caramelized upside-down apple tart
vacherin	ice cream and meringue cake

◆ **boissons** drinks

France produces a huge variety of excellent wines and you will not usually find wines from other countries in shops or on wine lists. Even very modest cafés will always offer wine with food. There are a number of French lagers and bottled light stouts available and cafés and brasseries will have draught lager. You can also find various types of beer from other countries, though UK-type draught beer and draught Guinness are generally only available in English and Irish pubs, of which there are many in bigger cities.

Normandy is famed for its cider. When accompanying a meal, especially in a pancake restaurant (**crêperie**), cider is often served in earthenware bowls.

People will often have a pre-meal drink (**apéritif**) and you will generally be offered one in a restaurant or if you are invited to eat in a French home. It is also quite common to invite friends in just for apéritifs and nibbles. Common apéritifs are whisky (**whisky**), port (**porto**), various sweet wines (**vins doux**), aniseed alcohols (**pastis**) and **kir** (white wine with blackcurrant liqueur).

Coffee is usually drunk after a meal. In someone's home you may be offered a herbal tea (**tisane**) as an alternative, particularly in the evening.

After-dinner drinks are always on offer in restaurants and vary little from those available in the UK, though fruit alcohols, often produced by small local distillers, are particularly prized in France.

FOOD AND DRINK GLOSSARY

abricot apricot
agneau lamb
aigre-doux sweet-and-sour
ail garlic
aïoli garlic mayonnaise
amande almond
ananas pineapple
anchois anchovy
anguille eel
aneth dill
arête fishbone
artichaut artichoke
asperges asparagus
assiette plate
aubergine aubergine
avocat avocado
bacon smoked back bacon
banane banana
bar sea bass
basilic basil
betterave beetroot
beurre doux/demi-sel unsalted/
   salted butter
bière beer
bifteck steak
bigorneaux winkles
blanc de poulet chicken breast
blettes Swiss chard
boîte de conserve can of food
boudin blanc white pudding
   (made with chicken or veal)
boudin noir black pudding
boulettes meatballs
brochet pike
brochette kebab
brocoli broccoli

brugnon nectarine
caille quail
cabillaud cod
calamar squid
canard duck
cannelle cinnamon
câpres capers
carotte carrot
cassis blackcurrants
céleri celery
cèpes ceps
cerises cherries
champignons mushrooms
champignons de Paris button
   mushrooms
chapon capon
châtaigne chestnut
chevreuil venison
chips (potato) crisps
chocolat chocolate
chou cabbage
chou-fleur cauliflower
choux de Bruxelles Brussels
   sprouts
ciboulette chives
cidre cider
citron lemon
citron vert lime
citrouille pumpkin
clous de girofle cloves
cœurs d'artichaut artichoke
   hearts
cognac brandy
colin hake, coley
concombre cucumber
congelé frozen

conservateur preservative
coquilles Saint-Jacques scallops
cornichons gherkins
côtelette cutlet
crabe crab
crème Chantilly sweetened whipped cream
crème fraîche thick, slightly soured fresh cream
crème pâtissière confectioner's custard
crêpe (de froment) (wholewheat) pancake
cresson cress
crevettes prawns
cuillère spoon, spoonful
cuillère à café teaspoon, teaspoonful
cuillère à soupe soup spoon, tablespoonful
cuillérée teaspoonful
cuisse de poulet chicken leg
daurade sea bream
déjeuner lunch
dessert dessert
dinde turkey
échalote shallot
écrevisses crayfish
édulcorant sweetener
églefin haddock
en conserve tinned, preserved
endives chicory
épice spice
épinards spinach
estragon tarragon
faisan pheasant
farine flour
fenouil fennel
fèves broad beans

figue fig
filet fillet
flétan halibut
foie liver
four oven
fraises strawberries
framboises raspberries
frites French fries, chips
fromage cheese
fromage blanc fromage frais (thick yoghurt)
fruits de mer seafood
fruits rouges summer fruits (raspberry, strawberry, redcurrant etc)
galette (de blé noir/de sarrasin) buckwheat pancake
garniture garnish, accompaniment
gâteau cake
girolles a type of wild mushroom
glace ice cream
gratin a dish, usually vegetable or fish, cooked and browned in a sauce in the oven
groseilles redcurrants
haddock smoked haddock
hareng herring
hareng fumé smoked herring
haricots verts green beans
huile oil
huile d'olive olive oil
huître oyster
jambon blanc, jambon cuit (cooked) ham
jambon cru/du pays/de Bayonne cured raw ham
lait milk
lait cru unpasteurized milk
lait demi-écrémé semi-skimmed milk

lait écrémé skimmed milk
lait entier full-cream milk
laitue round lettuce
langouste rock lobster
lapin rabbit
lard fumé/salé smoked/
unsmoked bacon
lardons small strips of bacon
laurier bayleaves
lentilles lentils
lièvre hare
limande lemon sole
lotte monkfish
maïs sweetcorn
maquereau mackerel
menthe mint
merguez spicy lamb or beef
sausages
merlan whiting
merlu hake
miel honey
morue salt cod
moules mussels
moutarde mustard
mûr ripe
mûres blackberries
myrtilles bilberries
navet turnip
noisettes hazelnuts
noix walnuts
noix de coco coconut
noix de muscade nutmeg
œuf egg
œuf à la coque boiled egg
œuf dur hard-boiled egg
œuf sur le plat fried egg
oignon onion
omelette omelette
orange orange

origan oregano
pain bread
pain au levain sourdough bread
pain au son bran bread
pain aux céréales wholegrain
bread
pain complet wholemeal bread
pain de campagne traditional
country bread
pain de mie sliced bread
pain de seigle rye bread
palourdes clams
parfum flavour
pastèque watermelon
pâte de coings quince paste
pâtes pasta
pêche peach
perdrix partridge
persil parsley
petit déjeuner breakfast
petits pois peas
pigeonneau young pigeon
pintade guinea fowl
piquant spicy
plat garni dish served with
vegetables
plat principal main dish
poêle frying pan
poire pear
poireau leek
pois chiches chickpeas
poisson fish
poivre pepper
poivre en grains peppercorns
poivron rouge/vert red/green
pepper
pomme apple
pomme de terre potato
porc pork

potiron pumpkin
poulet chicken
prune plum
pruneau prune
pudding heavy fruit sponge
purée mashed potato
radis radish
ragoût stew
raie skate
raisin grapes
raisins secs raisins, sultanas
repas meal
riz rice
rognons kidneys
romarin rosemary
rôti roast
rouget red mullet
safran saffron
saindoux lard
salé salted; savoury
sanglier wild boar
sardines sardines
sauce sauce
sauce béchamel white sauce
saucisse sausage

saucisson French salami
saumon salmon
sel salt
sirop fruit cordial, squash
sole (Dover) sole
sucre sugar
sucré sweet
surgelé frozen
truite trout
turbot turbot
thon tuna
thym thyme
tisane herbal tea
tomate tomato
tourte pie
tourteau crab
truite trout
veau veal
viande meat
viande hachée minced meat
vin (blanc/rouge/rosé) (white/red/rosé) wine
vinaigre vinegar
vinaigrette vinaigrette dressing

Nightlife in big cities in France is lively and at weekends can go on until the early hours. Bars close at around 2am, while clubs can stay open until at least 5am. A variety of live music can be found in bars and cafés, especially at weekends. In Paris, information on all cultural events and entertainments can be found in "l'Officiel des spectacles" or "Pariscope" (the latter also has information in English). Similar publications can be found in other big cities. These can be bought at newsagents and on news-stands.

If you want to go to the cinema, note that foreign-language films showing at big cinemas are often dubbed into French, while alternative cinemas frequently offer films in the original language, with subtitles in French. These are signalled **V.O.** (**version originale**) in programmes and outside the cinema. Cinemas, theatres and museums generally offer reduced rates for students and people over sixty. Students will be asked to show their student cards and over-sixties to produce evidence of age.

The basics

ballet	ballet *ba-lay*
band	groupe *groop*
bar	bar *bar*
cinema	cinéma *see-nay-ma*
circus	cirque *seerk*
classical music	musique classique *mU-zeek kla-seek*
club	boîte (de nuit) *bwat (duh nwee)*
concert	concert *kON-ser*
dubbed film	film doublé *feelm doo-blay*
festival	festival *fes-tee-val*
film	film *feelm*
folk music	musique traditionnelle *mU-zeek tra-dees-yoh-nel*
jazz	jazz *jaz*
modern dance	danse contemporaine *dONs kON-tON-poh-ren*
musical	comédie musicale *ko-may-dee mU-zee-kal*

party	(for a special occasion) **fête** fet, (in the evening)
	soirée swa-ray
pop music	pop pop
rock music	rock rok
show	spectacle spek-takl
subtitled film	film sous-titré feelm soo-tee-tray
theatre	théâtre tay-ahtr
ticket	billet bee-yay
to book	réserver ray-zer-vay
to go out	sortir sor-teer

SUGGESTIONS AND INVITATIONS

Expressing yourself

where can we go?
où est-ce qu'on pourrait aller ?
oo ess-kON poo-ray alay ?

shall we go for a drink?
on va prendre un verre ?
ON va prONdr AN ver ?

what do you want to do?
qu'est-ce que vous avez envie de faire ?
kess-kuh vooz avay ON-vee duh fer ?

what are you doing tonight?
qu'est-ce que vous faites ce soir ?
kess-kuh voo fet suh swar ?

would you like to …?
est-ce que vous aimeriez … ?
ess-kuh vooz ay-muhr-yay … ?

do you have plans?
est-ce que vous avez quelque chose de prévu ?
ess-kuh vooz avay kel-kuh-shohz duh pray-vU ?

we were thinking of going to …
on pensait aller à …
ON pON-se alay a …

I can't today, but maybe some other time
aujourd'hui, je ne peux pas, mais peut-être une autre fois
oh-zhoor-dwee, zhuh nuh puh pa, may puh-tetr Un oh-truh fwa

I'd love to
avec plaisir
avek play-zeer

I'm not sure I can make it
je ne suis pas sûr de pouvoir
zhuh nuh swee pa sUr duh poo-vwar

GOING OUT

ARRANGING TO MEET

Expressing yourself

what time shall we meet?
on se retrouve à quelle heure ?
ON suh ruh-troov a kel uhr ?

where shall we meet?
on se retrouve où ?
ON suh ruh-troov oo ?

would it be possible to meet a bit later?
est-ce qu'il serait possible de se retrouver un peu plus tard ?
ess-keel suh-ray poh-seebl duh suh ruh-troo-vay AN puh plU tar ?

I have to meet … at nine
j'ai rendez-vous avec … à neuf heures
zhay rON-day-voo avek … a nuhv uhr

I don't know where it is but I'll find it on the map
je ne sais pas où c'est mais je trouverai sur le plan
zhuh nuh say pa oo say may zhuh troo-vuh-ray sUr luh plON

see you tomorrow night
à demain soir
a duh-mAN swar

sorry I'm late
désolé d'être en retard
day-zoh-lay detr ON ruh-tar

I'll meet you later, I have to stop by the hotel first
je vous retrouverai plus tard, je dois d'abord passer à l'hôtel
zhuh voo ruh-troo-vuh-ray plU tar, zhuh dwa da-bor pa-say a loh-tel

I'll call/text you if there's a change of plan
je vous appelerai/vous enverrai un SMS s'il y a un changement
zhuh voo ra-peluh-ray/vooz ON-ve-ray AN ess-em-ess seel ya AN shONzh-mON

are you going to eat beforehand?
est-ce que vous aurez mangé avant ?
ess kuh vooz oh-ray mON-zhay avON ?

Understanding

ça vous va ?
is that OK with you?

on se retrouve là-bas
I'll meet you there

je viendrai vous chercher vers huit heures
I'll come and pick you up about 8

GOING OUT

63

on peut se retrouver devant …
we can meet outside …

**je vais vous donner mon numéro pour que vous m'appeliez
 demain**
I'll give you my number and you can call me tomorrow

Some informal expressions

aller boire un coup to go for a drink
prendre un pot to have a drink
manger un bout to have a bite to eat
branché trendy

FILMS, SHOWS AND CONCERTS

Expressing yourself

is there a guide to what's on?
est-ce qu'il y a un guide des spectacles ?
ess-keel ya AN geed day spek-takl ?

I'd like three tickets for …
je voudrais trois places pour …
zhuh voo-dray trwa plass poor …

two tickets, please
deux places, s'il vous plaît
duh plass, seel voo play

it's called …
ça s'appelle …
sa sa-pel …

I've seen the trailer
j'ai vu la bande-annonce
zhay vU la bON-da-nONs

what time does it start?
ça commence à quelle heure ?
sa koh-mONs a kel uhr ?

I'd like to go and see a show
je voudrais aller voir un spectacle
zhuh voo-dray alay wwar AN spek-takl

I'll find out whether there are still tickets available
je vais voir s'il reste des places
zhuh vay wwar seel rest day plass

do we need to book in advance?
est-ce qu'il faut réserver à l'avance ?
ess-keel foh ray-zer-vay a la-vONs ?

how long is it on for?
ça joue jusqu'à quand ?
sa zhoo zhUska kON ?

are there tickets for another day?
est-ce qu'il reste des places pour un autre jour ?
ess-keel rest day plass poor AN ohtr zhoor ?

I'd like to go to a bar with some live music
j'aimerais bien aller écouter de la musique dans un café
zhay-muh-ray byAN alay ay-koo-tay duh la mUzeek dONz AN ka-fay

what sort of music is it?
c'est quel genre de musique ?
say kel zhONr duh mU-zeek ?

are there any free concerts?
est-ce qu'il y a des concerts gratuits ?
ess-keel ya day kON-ser gra-twee ?

Understanding

guichet	box office
matinée	matinée
place sans visibilité	restricted view
réservations	bookings
séance	showing
sortie le …	on general release from …
VO (sous-titrée)	subtitles

c'est un concert en plein air
it's an open-air concert

il y a de très bonnes critiques
it's had very good reviews

ça sort la semaine prochaine
it comes out next week

ça joue à huit heures à l'UGC
it's on at 8pm at the UGC

il n'y a plus de places pour cette séance
that showing's sold out

c'est complet jusqu'au …
it's all booked up until …

ce n'est pas la peine de réserver
there's no need to book in advance

la pièce dure une heure et demie avec entracte
the play lasts an hour and a half, including the interval

prière d'éteindre votre portable
please turn off your mobile phones

PARTIES AND CLUBS

Expressing yourself

I'm having a little leaving party tonight
je fais une petite fête pour mon départ ce soir
zhuh fay Un puh-teet fet poor mON day-par suh swar

should I bring something to drink?
est-ce qu'il faut apporter quelque chose à boire ?
ess-keel foh a-por-tay kel-kuh-shohz a bwar ?

we could go to a club afterwards
on pourrait aller en boîte après
ON poo-ray alay ON bwat a-pray

do you have to pay to get in?
l'entrée est payante ?
lON-tray ay pay-yONt ?

I have to meet someone inside
je dois retrouver quelqu'un à l'intérieur
zhuh dwa ruh-troo-vay kel-kAN a lAN-tayr-yuhr

will you let me back in when I come back?
vous me laisserez entrer quand je reviens ?
voo muh lay-suh-ray ON-tray kON zhuh ruhv-yAN ?

the DJ's really cool
le DJ est top
luh dee-jay ay top

do you come here often?
tu viens souvent ici ?
tU vyAN soo-vON ee-see ?

can I buy you a drink?
je t'offre quelque chose à boire ?
zhuh tofr kel-kuh-shohz a bwar ?

thanks, but I'm with my boyfriend
merci, mais je suis avec mon copain
mer-see, may zhuh swee avek mON koh-pAN

no thanks, I don't smoke
non merci, je ne fume pas
nON mer-see, zhuh nuh fUm pa

Understanding

avec conso   first drink included
gratuit pour les filles ladies free up to midnight
 avant minuit
vestiaire   cloakroom

il y a une soirée chez Magali
there's a party at Magali's place

tu veux danser ?
do you want to dance?

je t'offre quelque chose à boire ?
can I buy you a drink?

est-ce que tu aurais du feu ?
have you got a light?

est-ce que tu aurais une cigarette ?
have you got a cigarette?

est-ce qu'on peut se revoir ?
can we see each other again?

je te raccompagne ?
can I see you home?

TOURISM AND SIGHTSEEING

France has an impressive range of museums and art galleries. Opening hours vary, but most are open from about 10am to 7pm. Some of the larger ones stay open late on Wednesdays or Thursdays. Note that local museums are closed on Mondays and national ones on Tuesdays (except for the Musée d'Orsay in Paris, which is closed on Mondays).

The best thing to do is to visit the local tourist information centre (**office de tourisme**), which will have up-to-date information on opening hours and closing days for the museums and monuments you are interested in. You will also find a range of leaflets on local places of interest, castles that are open to the public, maps and so on.

The basics

ancient	ancien *ONs-yAN*
antique	antique *ON-teek*
area	quartier *kar-tyay*
castle	château *sha-toh*
cathedral	cathédrale *ka-tay-dral*
century	siècle *syekl*
church	église *ay-gleez*
exhibition	exposition *eks-poh-zees-yON*
famous	célèbre *say-lebr*
gallery	galerie *gal-ree*
modern art	art moderne *ar moh-dern*
mosque	mosquée *mos-kay*
museum	musée *mU-zay*
painting	tableau *ta-bloh*
park	parc *park*
ruins	ruines *rween*
sculpture	sculpture *skUl-tUr*

statue	statue *sta-tU*
street map	plan (de la ville) *plON (duh la veel)*
synagogue	synagogue *see-na-gog*
tour guide	guide *geed*
tourist	touriste *too-reest*
tourist information centre	office de tourisme *oh-fees duh too-reezm*
town centre	centre-ville *sON-truh veel*

Expressing yourself

I'd like some information on …
j'aimerais avoir des renseignements sur …
zhay-muh-ray av-war day rON-sen-yuh-mON sUr …

can you tell me where the tourist information centre is?
pourriez-vous m'indiquer où est l'office de tourisme ?
poor-yay-voo mAN-dee-kay oo ay loh-fees duh too-reezm ?

do you have a street map of the town?
est-ce que vous auriez un plan de la ville ?
ess kuh vooz ohr-yay AN plON duh la veel ?

I was told there's an old abbey you can visit
on m'a dit qu'il y a une vieille abbaye qu'on peut visiter
ON ma dee keel ya Un vee-ey abay-ee kON puh vee-zee-tay

can you show me where it is on the map?
pourriez-vous me montrer où c'est sur le plan ?
poor-yay-voo muh mON-tray oo say sUr luh plON ?

how do you get there?
comment on y va ?
koh-mON ONn ee va ?

is it free?
c'est gratuit ?
say gra-twee ?

when was it built?
ça date de quand ?
sa dat duh kON ?

TOURISM, SIGHTSEEING

69

Understanding

en cours de rénovation	renovation work in progress
en cours de restauration	restoration work in progress
entrée libre	admission free
fermé	closed
ouvert	open
vieille ville	old town
visite guidée	guided tour
vous êtes ici	you are here *(on a map)*

il faut vous renseigner sur place
you'll have to ask when you get there

la prochaine visite guidée commence à 14 heures
the next guided tour starts at 2pm

MUSEUMS, EXHIBITIONS AND MONUMENTS

Expressing yourself

I've heard there's a very good ... exhibition on at the moment
il paraît qu'il y a une très bonne exposition sur ... en ce moment
eel pa-ray keel ya Un tray bon eks-poh-zees-yON sUr ... ON suh moh-mON

how much is it to get in?
combien coûte l'entrée ?
kON-byAN koot lON-tray ?

is there a charge for admission?
est-ce que l'entrée est payante ?
ess kuh lON-tray ay pay-yONt ?

is this ticket valid for the exhibition as well?
ce billet est-il valable aussi pour l'exposition (temporaire) ?
suh bee-yay et-eel va-labl oh-see poor leks-poh-zees-yON (tON-poh-rer) ?

are there any discounts for young people?
est-ce qu'il y a des réductions pour les jeunes ?
ess keel ya day ray-dUks-yON poor lay zhuhn ?

is it open on Sundays?
est-ce que c'est ouvert le dimanche ?
ess kuh sayt oo-ver luh dee-mONsh ?

two concessions and one full price, please
deux tarifs réduits et un plein tarif, s'il vous plaît
duh ta-reef ray-dwee ay AN plAN ta-reef, seel voo play

I have a student card
j'ai une carte d'étudiant
zhay Un kart day-tU-dyON

Understanding

audiophone	audioguide
billeterie	ticket office
exposition temporaire	temporary exhibition
exposition permanente	permanent exhibition
flash interdit	no flash photography
ne pas toucher, merci	please do not touch
photos interdites	no photography
plein tarif	full price
sens de la visite	this way
silence, s'il vous plaît	silence, please
tarif réduit	concession

l'entrée pour le musée coûte …
admission to the museum costs …

avec ce ticket, vous avez aussi accès à l'exposition
this ticket also allows you access to the exhibition

est-ce que vous avez une carte d'étudiant ?
do you have your student card?

GIVING YOUR IMPRESSIONS

Expressing yourself

it's beautiful
c'est magnifique
say ma-nee-feek

it was beautiful
c'était magnifique
say-tay ma-nee-feek

it's fantastic
c'est formidable
say for-mee-dabl

it was fantastic
c'était formidable
say-tay for-mee-dabl

I really enjoyed it
j'ai beaucoup aimé
zhay boh-koo ay-may

I didn't like it that much
je n'ai pas tellement aimé
zhuh nay pa tel-mON ay-may

it was a bit boring
c'était un peu ennuyeux
say-tay AN puh ON-nwee-yuh

it's very touristy
c'est très touristique
say tray too-rees-teek

I'm not really a fan of modern art
je ne suis pas vraiment fan d'art moderne
zhuh nuh swee pa vray-mON fan dar moh-dern

it's expensive for what it is
c'est cher pour ce que c'est
say sher poors kuh say

it was really crowded
il y avait énormément de monde
eel yavay ay-nor-may-mON duh mONd

we didn't go in the end, the queue was too long
finalement on n'y est pas allés, il y avait trop de queue
fee-nal-mON ON nee yay paz alay, eel yavay troh duh kuh

we didn't have time to see everything
on n'a pas eu le temps de tout voir
ON na paz U luh tON duh too vwar

Understanding

vous devriez vraiment aller voir …
you really must go and see …

je vous recommande d'aller à …
I recommend going to …

il y a une vue superbe sur toute la ville
there's a wonderful view over the whole city

c'est devenu un peu trop touristique
it's become a bit too touristy

la côte a été complètement défigurée
the coast has been completely ruined

SPORTS AND GAMES

France has the largest skiing area in the world, with over 8,000 km of slopes, making it a paradise for all winter sports (**sports d'hiver**) fans. There are ski resorts (**stations de ski**) in all the mountainous areas, although the main resorts are in the Alps and the Pyrenees.

The Atlantic coast offers great waters for surfing, especially in the French Basque country and the Landes region, but surfers also brave the chillier waters of Brittany and Normandy.

France's beautiful and varied landscape is a paradise for walkers. There is an excellent system of hiking paths (**sentiers de randonnée**), which are clearly marked and signposted: **PR** for **petite randonnée** (short distance, colour-coded yellow and white) and **GR** for **grande randonnée** (long-distance, colour-coded red and white). Maps and guides of these are available in local tourist offices (**offices de tourisme**) and also in newsagents. Cycling is also popular and mountain bikes (**VTT**, **vélo tout terrain**) can be hired in most towns and larger villages.

Rugby and football are two other French passions, France being amongst the top teams in the world for each sport. And, of course, there is the typically French sport of **pétanque** (bowls), which you will see played in many towns and villages in the country.

The basics

ball	*(large)* **ballon** ba-lON, *(small)* **balle** bal
basketball	**basket** ba-sket
bike	**vélo** vay-loh
board game	**jeu de société** zhuh duh soh-syay-tay
cards	**cartes** kart
chess	**échecs** ay-shek
cross-country skiing	**ski de fond** skee duh fON
downhill skiing	**ski alpin** skee alpAN
football	**football** foot-bol

hiking path	sentier de randonnée *sON-tyay duh rON-doh-nay*
match	match *match*
mountain biking	VTT *vay-tay-tay*
pool *(game)*	billard (américain) *bee-yar (a-may-ree-kAN)*
rugby	rugby *rUg-bee*
snowboarding	snowboard *snoh-bord*
sport	sport *spor*
surfing	surf *suhrf*
swimming	natation *na-ta-syON*
swimming pool	piscine *pee-seen*
table football	baby-foot *ba-bee foot*
tennis	tennis *tay-nees*
trip	excursion *eks-kUr-syON*
to go cycling	faire du vélo *fer dU vay-loh*
to go hiking	faire de la randonnée *fer duh la rON-doh-nay*
to have a game of ...	faire une partie de ... *fer Un par-tee duh ...*
to hire	louer *loo-ay*
to play	jouer à *zhoo-ay a*
to ski	skier *skee-yay*

Expressing yourself

are there ... lessons available?
est-ce qu'il y a des cours de ... ?
ess keel ya day koor duh ... ?

I'd like to hire ... for an hour
je voudrais louer ... pour une heure
zhuh voo-dray loo-ay ... poor Un uhr

how much is it per person per hour?
c'est combien par heure et par personne ?
say kON-byAN par uhr ay par per-son ?

I'm not very sporty
je ne suis pas très sportif
zhuh nuh swee pa tray spor-teef

I've never done it before
je n'en ai jamais fait
zhuh nONn ay zha-may fay

I've done it once or twice, a long time ago
j'en ai fait une ou deux fois, il y a longtemps
zhON ay fay Un oo duh fwa, eel ya lON-tON

I'm exhausted!
je suis épuisé !
zhuh sweez ay-pwee-zay !

we played …
on a joué à …
ON a zhoo-ay a …

I'd like to go and watch a football match
j'aimerais aller voir un match de foot
zhaym-ray alay vwar AN match duh foot

shall we stop for a picnic?
on s'arrête pour pique-niquer ?
ON sa-ret poor peek-nee-kay ?

Understanding

location de …   … for hire

**est-ce que vous avez des notions ou vous êtes complètement
débutant ?**
do you have any experience, or are you a complete beginner?

il faut verser une caution de …
there is a deposit of …

l'assurance est obligatoire et coûte …
insurance is compulsory and costs …

HIKING

Expressing yourself

are there any hiking paths around here?
est-ce qu'il y a des sentiers de randonnée par ici ?
ess keel ya day sON-tyay duh rON-doh-nay par ee-see ?

I'm looking for a guide to the hiking paths around here
je cherche un guide des sentiers de randonnée de la région
zhuh shersh AN geed day sON-tyay duh rON-doh-nay duh la rayzh-yON

I've heard there's a nice walk by the lake
il paraît qu'il y a une belle balade au bord du lac
eel pa-ray keel ya Un bel ba-lad oh bor dU lak

we're looking for a short walk somewhere round here
on cherche une petite balade à faire dans le coin
ON shersh Un puh-teet ba-lad a fer dON luh kwAN

how long does the hike take?   **is it very steep?**
combien dure la randonnée ?   ça monte beaucoup ?
kON-byAN dUr la rON-doh-nay ?   *sa mONt boh-koo ?*

where's the start of the path?   **is the path waymarked?**
où démarre le sentier ?   est-ce que le sentier est bien balisé ?
oo day-mar luh sON-tyay ?   *ess kuh luh sON-tyay ay byAN ba-lee-zay ?*

is it a circular path?
est-ce que c'est un sentier en boucle ?
ess kuh sayt AN sONt-yay ON bookl ?

Understanding

durée moyenne   average duration *(of walk)*

**c'est une randonnée d'environ trois heures sans compter les
 pauses**
it's about three hours' walk not including rest stops

prévoyez un K-Way® et des chaussures de randonnée
bring a waterproof jacket and walking shoes

SKIING AND SNOWBOARDING

Expressing yourself

I'd like to hire skis, poles and boots
je voudrais louer des skis, des bâtons et des chaussures de ski
zhuh voo-dray loo-ay day skee, day ba-tON ay day shoh-sUr duh skee

I'd like to hire a snowboard
je voudrais louer une planche de snowboard
zhuh voo-dray loo-ay Un plONsh duh snoh-bord

they're too big/small
elles sont trop grandes/petites
el sON troh grONd/puh-teet

a day pass
un forfait d'une journée
AN for-fay dUn zhoor-nay

I'm a complete beginner
je n'en ai jamais fait
zhuh nONn ay zha-may fay

Understanding

forfait	pass
remontée (mécanique)	ski lift
télésiège	chair lift
tire-fesses	T-bar, button lift

OTHER SPORTS

Expressing yourself

where can we hire bikes?
où est-ce qu'on peut louer des vélos ?
oo ess kON puh loo-ay day vay-loh ?

are there any cycle paths?
est-ce qu'il y a des pistes cyclables ?
ess keel ya day peestuh see-klabl ?

does anyone have a football?
est-ce que quelqu'un aurait un ballon de foot ?
ess kuh kel-kAN oh-ray AN ba-lON duh foot ?

which team do you support?
vous êtes pour quelle équipe ?
vooz et poor kel ay-keep ?

I support ...
je suis pour ...
zhuh swee poor ...

is there an open-air swimming pool?
est-ce qu'il y a une piscine en plein air ?
ess keel ya Un pee-seen ON plen er ?

I've never been diving before
je n'ai jamais fait de plongée
zhuh nay zha-may fay duh plON-zhay

I'd like to take beginners' sailing lessons
je voudrais prendre des cours de voile pour débutants
zhuh voo-dray prONdr day koor duh vwal poor day-bU-tON

I run for half an hour every morning
je cours tous les matins une demi-heure
zhuh koor too lay ma-tAN Un duh-mee uhr

what do I do if the kayak capsizes?
qu'est-ce que je fais si le kayak se renverse ?
kess kuh zhuh fay see luh ka-yak suh rON-vers ?

Understanding

il y a un court de tennis municipal près de la gare
there's a public tennis court not far from the station

le court de tennis est occupé
the tennis court's occupied

c'est la première fois que vous montez à cheval ?
is this the first time you've been horse-riding?

est-ce que vous savez nager ?
can you swim?

est-ce que tu joues au basket ?
do you play basketball?

INDOOR GAMES

Expressing yourself

it's your turn
c'est ton tour
say tON toor

shall we have a game of cards?
on se fait une partie de cartes ?
ON suh fay UN par-tee duh kart ?

does anyone know any good card games?
est-ce que quelqu'un connaît un bon jeu de cartes ?
ess kuh kel-kAN koh-nay AN bON zhuh duh kart ?

is anyone up for a game of Monopoly®?
ça vous dit de jouer au Monopoly® ?
sa voo dee duh zhoo-ay oh moh-noh-poh-lee ?

Understanding

est-ce que tu sais jouer aux échecs ?
do you know how to play chess?

est-ce que tu as un jeu de cartes ?
do you have a pack of cards?

Some informal expressions

je suis rétamé/crevé I'm knackered
il m'a écrasé he thrashed me

Traditionally, most shops in France are closed on Mondays. This is still true of many smaller shops, including butchers and many bakers. However, superstores (**grandes surfaces**) and the bigger supermarkets (**supermarchés**) are open on Mondays. Superstores stay open all day and until at least 8pm and are usually closed on Sundays. The majority of other shops close between 12 and 2 and butchers, bakers, greengrocers etc are usually closed until 3pm. Small shops close at 7pm, though in big cities you may find tiny grocery shops that stay open until around 10pm. You can usually find a baker's open on Sunday mornings until midday and in some places other food shops.

Open-air markets (**marchés**) are a colourful institution and can be found all over the country. In big cities there will usually be a central daily market. Small towns and villages will have a weekly market and in big cities there are numerous local markets with different opening days. Markets are a morning event. Stalls close down between midday and 1pm.

Payment by card is accepted in almost all shops although smaller ones may impose a minimum spend. You may be asked to type in your PIN number and may possibly be asked for ID. Otherwise, you just sign the receipt as in Britain.

Note that you can only buy cigarettes in state-licensed tobacconists (**bureaux de tabac**). These have a red lozenge-shaped sign, usually illuminated. They close at 7pm but a number of cafés are also licensed tobacconists and carry the lozenge sign.

Alcohol can be bought in supermarkets, grocery shops and specialist wine stores, but there is no equivalent of British off-licences that stay open late in the evening.

If you are buying a present of any sort, it is absolutely standard to have it gift-wrapped free of charge.

Some informal expressions

c'est de l'arnaque that's a rip-off
je n'ai pas un rond I'm skint
ça coûte les yeux de la tête it costs an arm and a leg

The basics

bakery	boulangerie *boo-lONzh-ree*
butcher's	boucherie *boosh-ree*
cash desk	caisse *kess*
cheap	pas cher *pa sher*, bon marché *bON mar-shay*
checkout	caisse *kess*
clothes	vêtements *vet-mON*
department store	grand magasin *grON ma-ga-zAN*
expensive	cher *sher*
gram	gramme *gram*
grocer's	épicerie *ay-pees-ree*
hypermarket	hypermarché *ee-per-mar-shay*
kilo	kilo *kee-loh*
present	cadeau *ka-doh*
price	prix *pree*
receipt	ticket de caisse *tee-kay duh kess*
sales	soldes *sold*
sales assistant	*(male)* vendeur *vON-duhr*, *(female)* vendeuse *vON-duhz*
shop	magasin *ma-ga-zAN*
shopping centre	centre commercial *sONtr koh-mers-yal*
souvenir	souvenir *soov-neer*
supermarket	supermarché *sUper-mar-shay*
to buy	acheter *ash-tay*
to cost	coûter *koo-tay*
to pay	payer *pay-yay*
to refund	rembourser *rON-boor-say*
to sell	vendre *vONdr*

Expressing yourself

is there a supermarket near here?
est-ce qu'il y a un supermarché par ici ?
ess keel ya AN sUper-mar-shay par ee-see ?

where can I buy cigarettes?
où est-ce que je peux acheter des cigarettes ?
oo ess kuh zhuh puh ash-tay day see-ga-ret ?

I'd like …
je voudrais …
zhuh voo-dray …

I'm looking for …
je cherche …
zhuh shersh …

do you sell …?
est-ce que vous avez … ?
ess kuh vooz avay … ?

do you know where I might find …?
savez-vous où je pourrais trouver … ?
sa-vay-voo oo zhuh poo-ray troo-vay … ?

can you order it for me?
est-ce que vous pouvez me le/la commander ?
ess kuh voo poo-vay muh luh/la koh-mON-day ?

how much is this?
ça coûte combien ?
sa koot kON-byAN ?

I'll take it
je le/la prends
zhuh luh/la prON

I haven't got much money
je n'ai pas beaucoup d'argent
zhuh nay pa boh-koo dar-zhON

I haven't got enough money
je n'ai pas assez d'argent
zhuh nay paz a-say dar-zhON

that's everything, thanks
ça sera tout, merci
sa suh-ra too, mer-see

can I have a (plastic) bag?
est-ce que je peux avoir un sac plastique ?
ess kuh zhuh puh av-war AN sak plas-teek ?

I think you've made a mistake with my change
je crois que vous avez fait une erreur en me rendant la monnaie
zhuh krwa kuh vooz avay fay Un ay-ruhr ON muh rON-dON la moh-nay

82

Understanding

fermé	closed
horaires (d'ouverture)	opening hours
nocturne le jeudi	late-night opening Thursdays
offre spéciale	special offer
ouvert	open
promotion	special offer
soldes	sales

et avec ceci ?
will there be anything else?

PAYING

Expressing yourself

where do I pay?
où est-ce qu'on paye ?
oo ess kON pey ?

how much do I owe you?
combien je vous dois ?
kON-byAN zh-voo dwa ?

could you write it down for me, please?
est-ce que vous pourriez me l'écrire, s'il vous plaît ?
ess kuh voo poor-yay muh lay-kreer, seel voo play ?

I'll pay in cash
je vais payer en liquide
zhuh vay pay-yay ON lee-keed

can I pay by credit card?
est-ce que je peux payer par carte ?
ess kuh zhuh puh pay-yay par kart ?

I'm sorry, I haven't got any change
je suis désolé, je n'ai pas du tout de monnaie
zhuh swee day-zoh-lay, zhuh nay pa dU too duh moh-nay

can I have a receipt?
est-ce que je peux avoir le ticket de caisse ?
ess kuh zhuh puh av-war luh tee-kay duh kess ?

Understanding

payez en caisse
pay at the cash desk

vous réglez comment ?
how would you like to pay?

SHOPPING

83

vous n'avez pas plus petit ?
do you have anything smaller?

je vais vous demander une pièce d'identité, s'il vous plaît
have you got any ID?

je vais vous demander une signature ici, s'il vous plaît
could you sign here, please?

FOOD

Expressing yourself

where can I buy food around here?
où est-ce que je peux acheter à manger par ici ?
oo ess kuh zhuh puh ash-tay a mON-zhay par ee-see ?

is there a market?
est-ce qu'il y a un marché ?
ess keel ya AN mar-shay ?

is there a bakery around here?
est-ce qu'il y a une boulangerie par ici ?
ess keel ya Un boo-lONzh-ree par ee-see ?

I'm looking for the cereal aisle
je cherche le rayon des céréales
zhuh shersh luh ray-yON day say-ray-al

I'd like five slices of ham
je voudrais cinq tranches de jambon
zhuh voo-dray sANk trONsh duh zhON-bON

I'd like some of that goat's cheese
je voudrais un peu de ce fromage de chèvre
zhuh voo-dray AN puh duh suh froh-mazh duh shevr

it's for four people
c'est pour quatre personnes
say poor kat per-son

about 300 grams
environ 300 grammes
ON-vee-rON trwa sON gram

a kilo of apples, please
un kilo de pommes, s'il vous plaît
AN kee-loh duh pom, seel voo play

a bit less
un peu moins
AN puh mwAN

a bit more
un peu plus
AN puh plUs

can I taste it?
est-ce qu'il serait possible de goûter ?
ess keel suh-ray poh-seebl duh goo-tay ?

does it travel well?
est-ce que ça peut voyager ?
ess kuh sa puh wwa-ya-zhay ?

Understanding

à consommer (de   best before …
  préférence) avant …
biologique   organic
maison   homemade
spécialités du pays   local specialities

il y a un marché tous les jours jusqu'à midi
there's a market every day until midday

il y a un épicier juste à côté qui reste ouvert tard le soir
there's a grocer's just round the corner that's open late

CLOTHES

Expressing yourself

I'm looking for the menswear section
je cherche le rayon hommes
zhuh shersh luh ray-yon om

can I try it on?
est-ce que je peux l'essayer ?
ess kuh zhuh puh lay-say-yay ?

no thanks, I'm just looking
non, merci, je regarde seulement
nON, mer-see, zhuh ruh-gard suhl-mON

I'd like to try the one in the window
je voudrais essayer celui/celle qui est en vitrine
zhuh voo-dray ay-say-yay suh-lwee/sel kee ay ON vee-treen

I take a size 39 *(in shoes)*
je fais du 39
zhuh fay dU trONt-nuhf

where are the changing rooms?
où sont les cabines d'essayage ?
oo sON lay ka-been day-say-yazh ?

it isn't quite right
ça ne me va pas
sa nuh muh va pa

it's too big/small
c'est trop grand/petit
say troh grON/puh-tee

do you have it in another colour?
est-ce que vous l'avez dans une autre couleur ?
ess kuh voo lavay dONz Un ohtr koo-luhr ?

do you have it in a smaller/bigger size?
est-ce que vous l'avez dans une plus petite/grande taille ?
ess kuh voo lavay dONz Un plU puh-teet/grONd ta-ee ?

do you have it in red?
est-ce que vous l'avez en rouge ?
ess kuh voo lavay ON roozh ?

yes, that's fine, I'll take it
oui, c'est bon, je le/la prends
wee, say bON, zhuh luh/la prON

no, I don't like it
non, je n'aime pas
nON, zhuh nem pa

I'll think about it
je vais réfléchir
zhuh vay ray-flay-sheer

I'd like to return this, it doesn't fit
je voudrais rendre ceci, ça ne va pas
zhuh voo-dray rONdr suh-see, sa nuh va pa

this ... has a hole in it, can I get a refund?
ce/cette ... a un trou, est-ce que je pourrais me faire rembourser ?
suh/set ... a AN troo, ess kuh zhuh poo-ray muh fer rON-boor-say ?

Understanding

cabines d'essayage   changing rooms
vêtements pour enfants   children's clothes
vêtements pour femmes   ladieswear
vêtements pour hommes   menswear

les articles en solde ne sont ni repris ni échangés
sale items cannot be returned or exchanged

bonjour, je peux vous aider ?
hello, can I help you?

nous ne l'avons qu'en bleu et en noir
we only have it in blue or black

il ne nous en reste plus dans cette taille
we don't have any left in that size

ça vous va bien
it suits you

c'est bien votre taille
it fits you really well

vous pouvez le/la rendre si ça ne va pas
you can bring it back if it doesn't fit

SOUVENIRS AND PRESENTS

Expressing yourself

I'm looking for a present to take home
je cherche un cadeau à ramener
zhuh shersh AN ka-doh a ram-nay

I'd like something that's easy to transport
je voudrais quelque chose de facile à transporter
zhuh voo-dray kel kuh shohz duh fa-seel a trONs-por-tay

it's for a little girl of four
c'est pour une petite fille de quatre ans
say poor Un puh-teet fee duh katr ON

could you gift-wrap it for me?
est-ce que vous pouvez me faire un paquet-cadeau ?
ess kuh voo poo-vay muh fer AN pa-kay ka-doh ?

Understanding

artisanal   traditionally made
fait main   handmade

combien êtes-vous prêt à dépenser ?
how much do you want to spend?

c'est pour offrir ?   **c'est typique de la région**
is it for a present?   it's typical of the region

The basics

black and white	(en) noir et blanc *(ON) nwar ay blON*
camera	appareil photo *a-pa-rey foto*
colour	(en) couleur *(ON) koo-luhr*
copy	exemplaire *eg-zON-pler*, retirage *ruh-tee-razh*
digital camera	appareil photo numérique *a-pa-rey foto nU-may-reek*
disposable camera	appareil photo jetable *a-pa-rey foto zhuh-tabl*
exposure	pose *pohz*
film	pellicule *pay-lee-kUl*
flash	flash *flash*
glossy	brillant *bree-yON*
matt	mat *mat*
memory card	carte mémoire *kart may-mwar*
negative	négatif *nay-ga-teef*
passport photo	photo d'identité *foto dee-dON-tee-tay*
photo	photo *foto*
photo booth	Photomaton® *foto-ma-tON*
reprint	retirage *ruh-tee-razh*
slide	diapositive *dya-poh-zee-teev*
to get photos developed	faire développer des photos *fer day-vlo-pay day foto*
to take a photo/photos	prendre une photo/des photos *prONdr Un foto/day foto*

Expressing yourself

could you take a photo of us, please?
est-ce que vous pourriez nous prendre une photo ?
ess-kuh voo poor-yay noo prONdr Un foto ?

you just have to press this button
il suffit d'appuyer sur ce bouton
eel sU-fee da-pwee-yay sUr suh boo-tON

I'd like a 200 ASA colour film
je voudrais une pellicule couleur 200 ASA
zhuh voo-dray Un pay-lee-kUl koo-luhr duh sON aza

do you have black and white films?
est-ce que vous avez des pellicules noir et blanc ?
ess-kuh vooz avay day pay-lee-kUl nwar ay blON ?

how much is it to develop a film of 36 photos?
combien coûte le développement d'une pellicule de 36 poses ?
kON-byAN koot luh day-vlop-mON dUn pay-lee-kUl duh trONt see pohz ?

I'd like to have this film developed
je voudrais faire développer cette pellicule
zhuh voo-dray fer day-vlo-pay set pay-lee-kUl

I'd like extra copies of some of the photos
je voudrais faire retirer certaines photos
zhuh voo-dray fer ruh-tee-ray ser-ten foto

three copies of this one and two of this one
trois exemplaires de cette photo et deux de celle-ci
trwaz eg-zON-pler duh set foto ay duh duh sel-see

can I print my digital photos here?
est-ce que vous développez les photos numériques ?
ess-kuh voo day-vlo-pay lay foto nU-may-reek ?

can you put these photos on a CD for me?
est-ce que vous pourriez mettre ces photos sur CD ?
ess-kuh voo poor-yay metr say foto sUr say-day ?

do you sell memory cards?
est-ce que vous avez des cartes mémoire ?
ess-kuh vooz avay day kart may-mwar ?

I've come to pick up my photos
je viens chercher mes photos
zhuh vyAN sher-shay may foto

I've got a problem with my camera
j'ai un problème avec mon appareil photo
zhay AN proh-blem avek mON a-pa-rey foto

I don't know what it is
je ne sais pas ce que c'est
zhuh nuh say pass kuh say

the flash doesn't work
le flash ne marche pas
luh flash nuh marsh pa

Understanding

développement en 1 heure	photos developed in one hour
format standard	standard format
photos sur CD	photos on CD
service express	express service

c'est peut-être la pile qui est morte
maybe the battery's dead

nous développons les photos numériques
we can print digital photos

c'est à quel nom ?
what's the name, please?

vous les voulez pour quand ?
when do you want them for?

on peut vous les développer en une heure
we can develop them in an hour

vos photos seront prêtes jeudi à partir de midi
your photos will be ready on Thursday at midday

BANKS

Banks in the Paris area are usually open from 10am to 5pm, Monday to Friday. In the rest of the country, they are open from Tuesday to Saturday and usually close for lunch between midday and 2pm. Some branches are open all day on Saturdays, some only in the morning. Many close early on the eve of a bank holiday. There are plenty of cashpoints (**distributeurs**) which take international cards, though your bank may charge you for withdrawals.

Not that French uses a comma rather than a dot for decimal points and that the euro symbol goes after the sum, so ten euros and fifteen cents is written 10,15€.

Some banks provide a currency exchange facility (**bureau de change**).

Some informal expressions
fric, thune cash
tirer du fric to get out some cash

The basics

bank	banque *bONk*
bank account	compte (bancaire) *kONt (bON-ker)*
banknote	billet *bee-yay*
bureau de change	bureau de change *bU-roh duh shONzh*
cashpoint	distributeur (automatique) *dees-tree-bU-tuhr (oh-toh-ma-teek)*
change	monnaie *moh-nay*
coin	pièce (de monnaie) *pee-yes (duh moh-nay)*
commission	commission *koh-mees-yON*
credit card	carte de crédit *kart duh kray-dee*
euro	euro *uh-roh*
(euro) cent	centime (d'euro) *sON-teem (duh-roh)*

PIN (number)	code confidentiel *kod kON-fee-dONs-yel*
pound *(currency)*	livre (sterling) *leev-ruh (ster-leeng)*
transfer	virement *veer-mON*
Travellers Cheque®	traveller's cheque® *trav-luhrz shek*, chèque de voyage *shek duh vwa-yazh*
withdrawal	retrait *ruh-tre*
to change	changer *shON-zhay*
to withdraw	retirer *ruh-tee-ray*

Expressing yourself

where I can get some money changed?
où est-ce que je peux changer de l'argent ?
oo ess-kuh zhuh puh shON-zhay duh lar-zhON ?

are banks open on Saturdays?
les banques sont-elles ouvertes le samedi ?
lay bONk sONt-el oo-vert luh sam-dee ?

I'm looking for a cashpoint
je cherche un distributeur
zhuh shersh AN dees-tree-bU-tuhr

I'd like to change £100
je voudrais changer 100 livres (sterling)
zhuh voo-dray shON-zhay sON leev-ruh (ster-leeng)

what commission do you charge?
qu'est que vous prenez comme commission ?
kess-kuh voo pruh-nay kom koh-mees-yON ?

I'd like to transfer some money
je voudrais faire un virement
zhuh voo-dray fer AN veer-mON

the cashpoint has swallowed my card
le distributeur a avalé ma carte
luh dees-tree-bU-tuhr a ava-lay ma kart

Understanding

composez votre code confidentiel puis validez
please enter your PIN number and press enter

autre montant
other amount

souhaitez-vous un ticket ?
would you like a receipt?

pour obtenir vos billets veuillez reprendre votre carte
please remove your card and wait for your cash

hors service
out of service

BANKS

POST OFFICES

Postboxes in France are yellow and collection times are displayed on the box. Outside the post office (**bureau de poste**) there are usually two boxes, one for local mail with the name of the city or area and one for all other destinations (**autres destinations**). Stamps can be bought in post offices and tobacconists (**bureau de tabac**). The price for a stamp for the UK and other European countries is the same as for France. For other destinations, you should go to a post office. Most post offices are open Monday to Friday from 9am to 5pm. In small towns they close between midday and 2pm. They are open from 9am to midday on Saturdays.

The basics

airmail	par avion *par av-yON*
envelope	enveloppe *ONv-lop*
letter	lettre *letr*
mail	courrier *koor-yay*
parcel	colis *koh-lee*, paquet *pa-kay*
post	poste *post*
postbox	boîte aux lettres *bwat oh letr*
postcard	carte postale *kart pohs-tal*
postcode	code postal *kod pohs-tal*
post office	(bureau de) poste *(bU-roh duh) post*
stamp	timbre *tANbr*
to post	poster *pos-tay*
to send	envoyer *ON-vwa-yay*
to write	écrire *ay-kreer*

Expressing yourself

is there a post office around here?
est-ce qu'il y a un bureau de poste par ici ?
es keel ya AN bU-roh duh post par ee-see ?

is there a postbox near here?
est-ce qu'il y a une boîte aux lettres près d'ici ?
ess keel ya Un bwat oh letr pray dee-see ?

what time does the post office close?
à quelle heure ferme la poste ?
a kel uhr ferm la post ?

do you sell stamps?
est-ce que vous vendez des timbres ?
ess kuh voo vON-day day tANbr ?

I'd like … stamps for the UK, please
je voudrais … timbres pour le Royaume-Uni, s'il vous plaît
zhuh voo-dray … tANbr poor luh rwa-yohm-Unee, seel voo play

I want to send this package by registered mail
je veux envoyer ce colis en recommandé
zhuh vuh ON-vwa-yay suh koh-lee ON ruh-koh-mON-day

how long will it take to arrive?
ça va mettre combien de temps pour arriver ?
sa va metr kON-byAN duh tON poor a-ree-vay ?

where can I buy envelopes?
où est-ce que je peux acheter des enveloppes ?
oo ess kuh zhuh puh ash-tay dayz ONv-lop ?

is there any post for me?
est-ce qu'il y a du courrier pour moi ?
ess keel ya dU koor-yay poor mwa ?

Understanding

dernière levée	last collection
destinataire	addressee, recipient
expéditeur	sender
première levée	first collection
recommandé	registered

ça met entre 3 et 5 jours
it'll take between three and five days

In France envelopes are addressed in much the same way as in the UK. However, if you are writing to someone in France, you should note that the postcode *precedes* the name of the town. The first two figures of the five-figure postcode indicate the department (**département**), ie the administrative area (07 in the address below is the code for the département Ardèche so it is not necessary to write "Ardèche" in the address). Here is a typical address:

Mme Céline Constantin
23 rue des Acacias
07440 Lamastre
France

The sender's address should be written on the back of the envelope at the top. Note that letters addressed to a country outside France must have the country name written in French. So, for the UK, **Royaume-Uni**.

The following abbreviations are commonly used in addresses:

Av (= **avenue**) avenue
Bd (= **boulevard**) boulevard
B.P. (= **boîte postale**) PO box
Dest. (= **destinataire**) addressee, recipient
Exp. (= **expéditeur**) sender
Pl (= **place**) square
r. (= **rue**) street
rte (= **route**) road

INTERNET CAFÉS AND E-MAIL

The number of internet cafés (**cafés Internet**) in France is increasing rapidly. Internet use is widespread, and it is common practice to swap e-mail addresses with people. Note that the French use an AZERTY keyboard, the layout of which differs from the QWERTY one you will be familiar with.

An "at" sign is called **une arobase**, a dot is **un point** and a hyphen is **un tiret**. If part of the address is written as all one word, you say **en un seul mot**. For example, jeandelhourme@wanadoo.fr would read as "**jean delhourme (en un seul mot) arobase wanadoo point F R**".

The basics

at sign	arobase *a-roh-baz*
e-mail	e-mail *ee-meyl*
e-mail address	adresse e-mail *a-dres ee-meyl*
Internet café	café Internet *ka-fay AN-ter-net*
key	touche *toosh*
keyboard	clavier *kla-vyay*
password	mot de passe *moh duh pas*
to copy	copier *koh-pyay*
to cut	couper *koo-pay*
to delete	supprimer *sU-pree-may*
to download	télécharger *tay-lay-shar-zhay*
to e-mail somebody	envoyer un e-mail à quelqu'un *ON-vwa-yay AN nee-meyl a kel-kAN*
to paste	coller *koh-lay*
to receive	recevoir *ruh-suh-vwar*
to save	sauvegarder *sohv-gar-day*
to send	envoyer *ON-vwa-yay*

Expressing yourself

is there an Internet café near here?
est-ce qu'il y a un café Internet près d'ici ?
ess keel ya AN ka-fay AN-ter-net pray dee-see ?

do you have an e-mail address?
est-ce que vous avez une adresse e-mail ?
ess kuh vooz avay Un a-dres ee-meyl ?

how do I get online?
qu'est-ce que je dois faire pour me connecter ?
kess kuh zhuh dwa fer poor muh koh-nek-tay ?

I'd just like to check my e-mails
je voudrais juste consulter mes e-mails
zhuh voo-dray jUst kON-sUl-tay mayz ee-meyl

would you mind helping me, I'm not sure what to do
est-ce que vous pourriez m'aider, je ne sais pas vraiment ce qu'il faut faire
ess kuh voo poor-yay may-day, zhuh nuh say pa vray-mON suh keel foh fer

I can't find the at sign on this keyboard
je ne trouve pas l'arobase sur ce clavier
zhuh nuh troov pa la-roh-baz sUr suh kla-vyay

it's not working
ça ne marche pas
sa nuh marsh pa

there's something wrong with the computer, it's frozen
il y a quelque chose qui ne va pas, l'ordinateur est bloqué
eel ya kel-kuh shohz kee nuh va pa, lor-dee-na-tuhr ay bloh-kay

how much will it be for half an hour?
ça coûte combien pour une demi-heure ?
sa koot kON-byAN poor Un duh-mee-uhr ?

when do I pay?
quand est-ce que je dois payer ?
kONt ess kuh zhuh dwa pay-yay ?

Understanding

boîte d'envoi   outbox
boîte de réception   inbox

il y a environ 20 minutes d'attente
you'll have to wait for 20 minutes or so

n'hésitez pas à demander si vous ne savez pas ce qu'il faut faire
just ask if you're not sure what to do

il vous suffit de taper votre mot de passe pour vous connecter
just enter this password to log on

INTERNET CAFÉS, E-MAIL

Public telephones have their own numbers, as in the UK, so you can receive as well as make calls there. All phoneboxes take phonecards (**Télécartes®**) and most now accept credit cards. Phoneboxes that take coins (**pièces**) are now extremely rare.

Phonecards are sold in tobacconists (**bureaux de tabac**), post offices (**bureaux de poste**), souvenir shops and other retail outlets. You can also buy prepaid cards (**cartes prépayées**).

Phone numbers in France have 10 digits and always start with a 0. Note that the way of giving a French telephone number is to use double figures, so, for the number 04.75.06.30.51, a person will say: zéro quatre, soixante-quinze, zéro six, trente, cinquante et un.

The France Telecom number for directory enquiries is **12**. Note that if you are using a British mobile phone to call someone in France, you need to add the country code from Britain (0033), then omit the zero from the beginning of the French number. When phoning Britain, you don't need any international code.

To call the UK from a French landline, dial 00 44 followed by the full phone number, minus the first zero of the area code. To dial France from the UK, dial 00 33 and drop the first zero of the phone number.

The basics

answering machine	répondeur *ray-pON-duhr*
call	appel *a-pel*
directory enquiries	renseignements *rON-sen-yuh-mON*
hello	allô *a-loh*
international call	appel international *a-pel AN-ter-nas-yoh-nal*
local call	appel local *a-pel loh-kal*
message	message *may-sazh*
mobile	portable *por-tabl*

national call	appel national *a-pel nas-yoh-nal*
phone	téléphone *tay-lay-fon*
phone book	annuaire *a-nU-er*
phone box	cabine téléphonique *ka-been tay-lay-fo-neek*
phone call	appel *a-pel*
phonecard	carte de téléphone *kart duh tay-lay-fon*, Télécarte® *tay-lay-kart*
phone number	numéro de téléphone *nU-may-roh duh tay-lay-fon*
ringtone	sonnerie *so-ne-ree*
text message	SMS *es-em-es*
Yellow Pages®	Pages Jaunes® *pazh zhohn*
to call somebody	appeler quelqu'un *a-play kel-kAN*
to phone somebody	téléphoner à quelqu'un *tay-lay-fo-nay a kel-kAN*
to recharge	recharger *ruh-shar-zhay*
to text somebody	envoyer un SMS à quelqu'un *ON-vwa-yay UN es-em-es a kel-kAN*

Expressing yourself

where can I buy a phonecard?
où est-ce que je peux acheter une carte de téléphone ?
oo ess kuh zhuh puh ash-tay Un kart duh tay-lay-fon ?

I'd like to make a reverse-charge call
je voudrais appeler en PCV
zhuh voo-dray a-play ON pay-say-vay

is there a phone box near here, please?
excusez-moi, est-ce qu'il y a une cabine téléphonique près d'ici ?
eks-kU-zay-mwa, ess keel ya Un ka-been tay-lay-fo-neek pray dee-see ?

can I plug my phone in here to recharge it?
est-ce que je peux brancher mon portable ici pour le recharger ?
ess kuh zhuh puh brON-shay mON por-tabl ee-see poor luh ruh-shar-zhay ?

do you have a mobile number?
est-ce que vous avez un numéro de portable ?
ess kuh vooz a-vay AN nU-may-roh duh por-tabl ?

where can I contact you?
où est-ce que je peux vous joindre ?
oo ess kuh zhuh puh voo zhwANdr ?

did you get my message?
avez-vous eu mon message ?
a-vay voo U mON may-sazh ?

le numéro que vous avez demandé n'est pas attribué
the number you have dialled has not been recognized

appuyez sur la touche dièse/étoile
please press the hash/star key

MAKING A CALL

Expressing yourself

hello, this is David Brown (speaking)
allô, bonjour, David Brown à l'appareil
a-loh, bON-zhoor, David Brown a la-pa-rey

hello, could I speak to…, please?
allô, bonjour, est-ce que je pourrais parler à … ?
a-loh, bON-zhoor, ess kuh zhuh poo-ray par-lay a … ?

hello, is that Caroline?
allô, Caroline ?
a-loh, ka-roh-leen ?

do you speak English?
est-ce que vous parlez anglais ?
ess kuh voo par-lay ON-glay ?

could you speak more slowly, please?
est-ce que vous pourriez parler plus lentement, s'il vous plaît ?
ess kuh voo poor-yay par-lay plU lON-tuh-mON, seel voo play ?

I can't hear you, could you speak up, please?
je ne vous entends pas bien, est-ce que vous pourriez parler plus fort ?
zhuh nuh vooz ON-tON pa byAN, ess kuh voo poor-yay par-lay plU for ?

TELEPHONE

could you tell him/her I called?
est-ce que vous pourriez lui dire que j'ai appelé ?
ess kuh voo poor-yay lwee deer kuh zhay a-play ?

could you ask him/her to call me back?
est-ce que vous pourriez lui dire de me rappeler ?
ess kuh voo poor-yay lwee deer duh muh ra-play ?

I'll call back later
je rappellerai plus tard
zhuh ra-pel-ray plU tar

thank you, goodbye
merci, au revoir
mer-see, oh ruh-vwar

my name is … and my number is …
je suis … et mon numéro est le …
zhuh swee … ay mON nU-may-roh ay luh …

do you know when he/she might be available?
est-ce que vous savez quand je pourrai le/la joindre ?
ess kuh voo sa-vay kON zhuh poo-ray luh/la zhwANdr ?

Understanding

qui est à l'appareil ?
who's calling?

un instant, s'il vous plaît
hold on

vous vous êtes trompé de numéro
you've got the wrong number

il/elle n'est pas là pour le moment
he's/she's not here at the moment

est-ce que vous voulez laisser un message ?
do you want to leave a message?

je lui dirai que vous avez appelé
I'll tell him/her you called

je lui dirai de vous rappeler
I'll ask him/her to call you back

je vous le/la passe
I'll just hand you over to him/her

PROBLEMS

Expressing yourself

I don't know the code
je ne connais pas l'indicatif
zhuh nuh ko-nay pa lAN-dee-ka-teef

it's engaged
ça sonne occupé
sa son oh-kU-pay

there's no reply
il n'y a personne
eel nya per-son

I couldn't get through
je n'ai pas réussi à le/la joindre
zhuh nay pa ray-U-see a luh/la zhwANdr

I don't have much credit left on my phone
il ne me reste plus beaucoup de crédit sur mon portable
eel nuh muh rest plU boh-koo duh kray-dee sUr mON por-tabl

we're about to get cut off
ça va couper
sa va koo-pay

the reception's really bad
il y a une très mauvaise réception
eel ya Un tray moh-vez ray-seps-yON

I can't get a signal
il n'y a pas de réception
eel nya pa duh ray-seps-yON

Some informal expressions

passer un coup de fil à quelqu'un to give somebody a ring
elle m'a raccroché au nez she hung up on me

If you are an EU national, pick up an E I I I form from the Post Office before you go to France. This ensures that the cost of any medical treatment you may need in France will be refunded to you when you return home, on production of a receipt.

You can visit a health centre (**centre médical**) or a medical practice (**cabinet médical**). Also, in serious cases, you can go to a hospital casualty department (**urgences**). Doctors can be either **conventionné** (working for the national health service and charging set rates) or private. The phone number for the emergency medical services (**SAMU**) is **15**. You can find a list of general practitioners in the Yellow Pages® of the telephone directory (**annuaire**) for your area. Look up the heading **Médecins** then **Médecine générale**, then the town or village where you are. On Sundays and after hours, the name and telephone number of the duty doctor (**médecin de garde**) is posted outside surgeries. In the Yellow Pages®, specialists and practitioners of alternative medicine are listed after general practitioners, in order of specialization.

Medicines can only be bought from a chemist's (**pharmacie**). This includes over the counter medicines like aspirin and paracetamol. Chemists are open from 9am to 7 or 8pm from Monday to Saturday, though many close between midday and 2pm. After hours there is always a duty pharmacy (**pharmacie de garde**) open in the area.

The basics

allergy	allergie *a-ler-zhee*
ambulance	ambulance *ON-bU-lONs*
aspirin	aspirine *as-pee-reen*
blood	sang *sON*
broken	cassé *ka-say*
casualty (department)	urgences *Ur-zhONs*
chemist's	pharmacie *far-ma-see*
condom	préservatif *pray-zer-va-teef*

dentist	dentiste *dON-teest*
diarrhoea	diarrhée *dya-ray*
doctor	médecin *mayd-sAN*
food poisoning	intoxication alimentaire *AN-tok-see-kas-yON a-lee-mON-ter*
GP	(médecin) généraliste *(mayd-sAN) zhay-nay-ra-leest*
gynaecologist	gynécologue *zhee-nay-koh-log*
hospital	hôpital *oh-pee-tal*
infection	infection *AN-feks-yON*
medicine	médicament *may-dee-ka-mON*
optician	opticien *op-tees-yAN*
painkiller	calmant *kal-mON*
period(s)	règles *regl*
plaster	pansement *pONs-mON*
prescription	ordonnance *or-doh-nONs*
rash	éruption cutanée *ay-rUps-yON kU-ta-nay*
spot	bouton *boo-tON*
sunburn	coup de soleil *koo duh soh-ley*
surgical spirit	alcool à 90°C *al-kol a kat-ruh vAN dees*
tablet	comprimé *kON-pree-may*
temperature	fièvre *fee-yevr*
vaccination	vaccin *vak-sAN*
x-ray	radio *ra-dyoh*
to disinfect	désinfecter *day-zAN-fek-tay*
to faint	s'évanouir *say-va-nweer*
to vomit	vomir *voh-meer*

Expressing yourself

does anyone have an aspirin/a tampon/a plaster, by any chance?
est-ce que quelqu'un aurait une aspirine/un tampon/un pansement par hasard ?
ess kuh kel-kAN oh-ray UN as-pee-reen/AN tON-pON/AN pONs-mON par a-zar ?

I need to see a doctor
il faut que j'aille voir un médecin
eel foh kuh zha-ee vwar AN mayd-sAN

where can I find a doctor?
où est-ce que je peux trouver un médecin ?
oo ess kuh zhuh puh troo-vay AN mayd-sAN ?

I'd like to make an appointment for today
je voudrais prendre rendez-vous pour aujourd'hui
zhu voo-dray prONdr rON-day-voo poor oh-zhoor-dwee

as soon as possible
le plus tôt possible
luh plU toh poh-seebl

can you send an ambulance to …
est-ce que vous pourriez faire venir une ambulance à/au …
ess kuh voo poor-yay fer vuh-neer Un ON-bU-lONs a/oh …

I've lost a contact lens	**I've broken my glasses**
j'ai perdu une lentille	j'ai cassé mes lunettes
zhay per-dU UN lON-tee	*zhay ka-say may lU-net*

Understanding

cabinet médical	doctor's surgery
salle d'attente	waiting room
urgences	casualty department

il n'y a rien de libre avant jeudi
there are no appointments available until Thursday

vendredi à 14 heures, ça vous va ?
is Friday at 2pm OK?

AT THE DOCTOR'S OR THE HOSPITAL

Expressing yourself

I have an appointment with Dr …
j'ai rendez-vous avec le Docteur …
zhay rON-day-voo a-vek luh dok-tuhr …

I don't feel very well	**I feel very weak**
je me sens pas très bien	je me sens très faible
zhu nuh muh sON pa tray byAN	*zhu muh sON tray febl*

I don't know what it is
je ne sais pas ce que c'est
zhuh nuh say pas kuh say

I've got a headache
j'ai mal à la tête
zhay mal a la tet

I've got a sore throat
j'ai mal à la gorge
zhay mal a la gorzh

it hurts
ça fait mal
sa fay mal

I feel sick
j'ai mal au cœur
zhay mal oh kuhr

it's been three days
ça fait trois jours
sa fay trwa zhoor

I've been bitten/stung by …
j'ai été mordu/piqué par …
zhay ay-tay mor-dU/pee-kay par …

I've got toothache/stomachache
j'ai mal aux dents/au ventre
zhay mal oh dON/oh vONtr

my back hurts
j'ai mal au dos
zhay mal oh doh

it hurts here
ça fait mal ici
sa fay mal ee-see

it's got worse
ça s'est aggravé
sa say a-gra-vay

it started last night
ça a commencé la nuit dernière
sa a koh-mON-say la nwee der-nyer

it's never happened to me before
ça ne m'était jamais arrivé avant
sa ne may-tay zha-may a-ree-vay a-vON

I've got a temperature
j'ai de la fièvre
zhay duh la fee-yevr

I have asthma
j'ai de l'asthme
zhay duh lasm

I have a heart condition
je suis cardiaque
zhuh swee kar-dyak

I've been on antibiotics for a week and I'm not getting any better
je suis sous antibiotiques depuis une semaine et ça ne va pas mieux
zhuh swee sooz ON-tee-byoh-teek duh-pwee Un suh-men ay sa nuh va pa myuh

it itches
ça démange
sa day-mONzh

I'm on the pill
je prends la pilule
zhuh prON la pee-lUl

I'm ... months pregnant
je suis enceinte de ... mois
zhuh sweez ON-sANt duh ... mwa

I've had a blackout
je me suis évanoui
zhuh muh sweez ay-va-nwee

I'm allergic to penicillin
je suis allergique à la pénicilline
zhuh sweez a-ler-zheek a la pay-nee-see-leen

I've twisted my ankle
je me suis tordu la cheville
zhuh muh swee tor-dU la shuh-vee

I fell and hurt my back
je suis tombé sur le dos
zhuh swee tON-bay sUr luh doh

I've lost a filling
j'ai perdu un plombage
zhay per-dU AN plON-bazh

is it serious?
c'est grave ?
say grav ?

is it contagious?
c'est contagieux ?
say kON-ta-zhyuh ?

how is he/she?
comment va-t-il/va-t-elle ?
koh-mON va-teel/va-tel ?

how much do I owe you?
combien je vous dois ?
kON-byAN zh-voo dwa ?

Understanding

si vous voulez bien patientez dans la salle d'attente ...
if you'd like to take a seat in the waiting room ...

où est-ce que vous avez mal ?
where does it hurt?

respirez bien fort
take a deep breath

allongez-vous, s'il vous plaît
lie down, please

êtes-vous allergique à ... ?
are you allergic to ...?

est-ce que ça fait mal quand j'appuie ici ?
does it hurt when I press here?

est-ce que vous êtes vacciné contre ... ?
have you been vaccinated against ...?

avez-vous des traitements en cours ?
are you taking any other medication?

je vais vous faire une ordonnance
I'm going to write you a prescription

ça devrait passer en quelques jours
it should clear up in a few days

ça devrait cicatriser rapidement
it should heal quickly

il va falloir opérer
you're going to need an operation

revenez me voir dans une semaine
come back and see me in a week

AT THE CHEMIST'S

Expressing yourself

I'd like a box of plasters, please
je voudrais une boîte de pansements, s'il vous plaît
zhuh voo-dray Un bwat duh pONs-mON, seel voo play

could I have something for a bad cold?
est-ce que vous pourriez me donner quelque chose contre le rhume ?
ess kuh voo poor-yay muh doh-nay kel-kuh shohz kON-truh luh rUm ?

I need something for a cough
j'ai besoin de quelque chose contre la toux
zhay buh-zwAN duh kel-kuh shohz kON-truh la too

I'm allergic to aspirin
je suis allergique à l'aspirine
zhuh sweez a-ler-zheek a las-pee-reen

I need the morning-after pill
j'aurais besoin de la pilule du lendemain
zhoh-ray buh-zwAN duh la pee-lUl dU lON-duh-mAN

I'd like to try a homeopathic remedy
je voudrais essayer de prendre de l'homéopathie
zhuh voo-dray ay-say-yay duh prONdr duh loh-may-oh-pa-tee

I'd like a bottle of solution for soft contact lenses
je voudrais une solution de nettoyage pour lentilles souples
zhuh voo-dray Un soh-lUs-yON duh nay-twa-yazh poor lOn-tee soopl

Understanding

appliquer	apply
à prendre trois fois par jour avant les repas	take three times a day before meals
comprimé	tablet
contre-indications	contra-indications
crème	cream
effervescent	effervescent
effets secondaires éventuels	possible side effects
en poudre	powder
gélule	capsule
notice	directions for use
podologie	dosage
pommade	ointment
sirop	syrup
suppositoires	suppositories
uniquement sur ordonnance	available on prescription only

Some informal expressions

être cloué au lit to be stuck in bed
tomber dans les pommes to pass out
être patraque to feel under the weather
être barbouillé to feel queasy

HEALTH

PROBLEMS AND EMERGENCIES

Look out for pickpockets, particularly in tourist areas.

If you lose something in a station etc, go to lost property (**objets trouvés**). Otherwise go to the nearest police station (**commissariat** or **gendarmerie**).

In an emergency, dial **17** for **police secours**, a centralized service which takes calls and coordinates the appropriate response. The police in France wear dark blue uniforms and are divided into various services with different responsibilities. To call the fire brigade (**pompiers**), dial **18**. Dial **15** for emergency medical services (**SAMU**).

The basics

accident	accident *ak-see-dON*
ambulance	ambulance *ON-bU-lONs*
coastguard	gendarmerie maritime *zhON-dar-muh-ree ma-ree-teem*
disabled	handicapé *ON-dee-ka-pay*
doctor	médecin *mayd-sAN*
emergency	urgence *Ur-zhONs*
fire brigade	pompiers *pON-pyay*
hospital	hôpital *oh-pee-tal*
ill	malade *ma-lad*
injured	blessé *blay-say*
police	police *poh-lees*

Expressing yourself

can you help me?
est-ce que vous pourriez m'aider ?
ess kuh voo poor-yay may-day ?

help!
au secours !
ohs-koor !

be careful!
attention !
a-tONs-yON !

it's an emergency!
c'est urgent !
set Ur-zhON !

there's been an accident
il y a eu un accident
eel ya U ANn ak-see-dON

could I use your mobile, please?
excusez-moi, est-ce que je pourrais utiliser votre portable ?
eks-kU-zay mwa, ess kuh zhuh poo-ray U-tee-lee-zay vo-truh por-tabl ?

does anyone here speak English?
est-ce que quelqu'un parle anglais ?
ess kuh kel-kAN parl ON-glay ?

I need to contact the British consulate
je dois contacter le consulat britannique
zhuh dwa kON-tak-tay luh kON-sU-la bree-ta-neek

where's the nearest police station?
où est le commissariat le plus proche ?
oo ay luh koh-mee-sa-rya luh plU prosh ?

what do I have to do?
qu'est-ce que je dois faire ?
kess kuh zhuh dwa fer ?

my bag's been stolen
on m'a volé mon sac
ON ma voh-lay mON sak

my passport/credit card has been stolen
on m'a volé mon passeport/ma carte de crédit
ON ma voh-lay mON pas-por/ma kart duh kray-dee

I've lost …
j'ai perdu …
zhay per-dU …

I've been attacked
j'ai été agressé
zhay ay-tay a-gray-say

my son/daughter is missing
mon fils/ma fille a disparu
mON fees/ma fee a dees-pa-rU

I've broken down
je suis en panne
zhuh sweez ON pan

my car's been towed away
ma voiture a été emmenée à la fourrière
ma vwa-tUr a ay-tay ONm-nay a la foo-ryer

my car's been broken into
on a forcé la porte/le coffre de ma voiture
ONn a for-say la port/luh kofr duh ma vwa-tUr

there's a man following me
il y a un homme qui me suit
eel ya ANn om kee muh swee

is there disabled access?
est-ce qu'il y a un accès pour handicapés ?
ess keel ya ANn ak-se poor ON-dee-ka-pay ?

can you keep an eye on my things for a minute?
pouvez-vous surveiller mes affaires un instant ?
poo-vay voo sUr-vay-yay mayz a-fer ANn AN-stON ?

Understanding

attention au chien	beware of the dog
commissariat	police station
gendarmerie	police station
objets trouvés	lost property
police-secours	police emergency services
SAMU	emergency medical services
secours de montagne	mountain rescue
service de dépannage	breakdown service
sortie de secours	emergency exit

POLICE

Expressing yourself

I want to report something stolen
je voudrais faire une déclaration de vol
zhuh voo-dray fer Un day-kla-ras-yON duh vol

I need a document from the police for my insurance company
j'ai besoin d'un certificat de police pour ma compagnie d'assurances
zhay buh-zwAN dAN ser-tee-fee-ka duh poh-lees poor ma kON-pa-nee da-sU-rONs

Understanding

Filling in forms

nom de famille surname
nom de jeune fille maiden name
prénoms first names
date de naissance date of birth
lieu de naissance place of birth
sexe: H/F sex: M/F
nationalité nationality
adresse address
code postal postcode
pays country
durée du séjour duration of stay
date d'arrivée/de départ arrival/departure date
profession occupation
numéro de passeport passport number

qu'est-ce qu'il vous manque ?
what's missing?

quand cela s'est-il passé ?
when did this happen?

où logez-vous ?
where are you staying?

pouvez-vous le/la décrire ?
can you describe him/her/it?

je vais vous demander de remplir ce formulaire
would you fill in this form, please?

une signature ici, s'il vous plaît
would you sign here, please?

Some informal expressions

flic cop
taule jail
on m'a piqué mon portefeuille my wallet's been nicked
il s'est fait pincer he got nicked

The basics

after	après *a-pray*
afternoon	après-midi *a-pray-mee-dee*
already	déjà *day-zha*
always	toujours *too-zhoor*
at lunchtime	à l'heure du déjeuner *a luhr dU day-zh-nay*
at the moment	en ce moment *ON suh moh-mON*
before	avant *a-vON*
between ... and ...	entre ... et ... *ONtr ... ay ...*
day	jour *zhoor*
during	pendant *pON-dON*
early	tôt *toh*
evening	soir *swar*
for a long time	longtemps *lON-tON*
from ... to ...	de ... à ... *duh ... a ...*
from time to time	de temps en temps *duh tONz ON tON*
in a little while	d'ici peu *dee-see puh*
in the evening	dans la soirée *dON la swa-ray*
last	dernier *der-nyay*
late	tard *tar*
morning	matin *ma-tAN*
month	mois *mwa*
never	jamais *zha-may*
next	prochain *pro-shAN*
night	nuit *nwee*
not yet	pas encore *paz ON-kor*
now	maintenant *mAN-tuh-nON*
occasionally	de temps en temps *duh tONz ON tON*
often	souvent *soo-vON*
rarely	rarement *rar-mON*
recently	récemment *ray-sa-mON*
since	depuis *duh-pwee*
sometimes	quelquefois *kel-kuh-fwa*
soon	bientôt *byAN-toh*
still	encore *ON-kor*, **toujours** *too-zhoor*

straightaway	tout de suite *toot sweet*
until	jusqu'à *zhUs-ka*
week	semaine *suh-men*
weekend	week-end *wee-kend*
year	an *ON*

Expressing yourself

see you soon!
à bientôt !
a byAN-toh !

see you later!
à plus tard !
a plU tar !

see you on Monday!
à lundi !
a lAN-dee !

have a good weekend!
bon week-end !
bON wee-kend !

sorry I'm late
désolé d'être en retard
day-zoh-lay detr ON ruh-tar

I haven't been there yet
je n'y ai pas encore été
zhuh ny-ay paz ON-kor ay-tay

I haven't had time to …
je n'ai pas eu le temps de …
zhuh nay paz U luh tON duh …

I've got plenty of time
j'ai tout mon temps
zhay too mON tON

I'm in a rush
je suis pressé
zhuh swee pray-say

hurry up!
dépêche-toi !/dépêchez-vous !
day-pesh-twa !/day-pay-shay voo !

just a minute, please
un instant, s'il vous plaît
ANn AN-stAN, seel voo play

I had a late night
je me suis couché tard
zhuh muh swee koo-shay tar

I got up very early
je me suis levé très tôt
zhuh muh swee luh-vay tray toh

I waited ages
j'ai attendu une éternité
zhay a-tON-dU Un ay-ter-nee-tay

I have to get up very early tomorrow to catch my plane
je dois me lever très tôt demain pour prendre l'avion
zhuh dwa muh luh-vay tray toh duh-mAN poor prONdr lav-yON

we only have four days left
il ne nous reste que quatre jours
eel nuh noo rest kuh katr zhoor

THE DATE

You can write the date in figures as in English eg 04/04/06. When written out in full with the day of the week or when spoken it is: **le dimanche quatre avril.** Note that French uses cardinal not ordinal numbers, so, in English "the fourth of April" and in French **le quatre avril.** The exception to this is the first of every month, where the ordinal is used: **le 1er mai** (**le premier mai**).

The basics

at the beginning of	au début de *oh day-bU duh*
at the end of	à la fin de *a la fAN duh*
in the middle of	en milieu de *ON meel-yuh duh*
in two days' time	dans deux jours *dON duh zhoor*
last night	hier soir *ee-yer swar*
the day after tomorrow	après-demain *a-pray duh-mAN*
the day before yesterday	avant-hier *a-vON tee-yer*
today	aujourd'hui *oh-zhoor-dwee*
tomorrow	demain *duh-mAN*
tomorrow morning/afternoon/ evening	demain matin/après-midi/soir *duh-mAN ma-tAN/a-pray-mee-dee/swar*
yesterday	hier *ee-yer*
yesterday morning/afternoon evening	hier matin/après-midi/soir *ee-yer ma-tAN/a-pray-mee-dee/swar*

Expressing yourself

I was born in 1975
je suis né en 1975
zhuh swee nay ON meel nuhf sON swa-sONt kANz

I came here a few years ago
je suis venu ici il y a quelques années
zhuh swee vuh-nU ee-see eel ya kel-kuhz a-nay

I spent a month in France last summer
j'ai passé un mois en France l'été dernier
zhay pa-say AN mwa ON frONs lay-tay der-nyay

TIME AND DATE

I was here last year at the same time
j'étais ici l'an dernier à la même époque
jay-tay ee-see lON der-nyay a la mem ay-pok

what's the date today?
on est le combien aujourd'hui ?
ONn ay luh kON-byAN oh-zhoor-dwee ?

what day is it today?
quel jour on est aujourd'hui ?
kel zhoor ONn ay oh-zhoor-dwee ?

it's the 1st of May
on est le premier mai
ONn ay luh pruh-myay may

I'm staying until Sunday
je suis ici jusqu'à dimanche
zhuh sweez ee-see zhUs-ka dee-mONsh

we're leaving tomorrow
nous partons demain
noo par-tON duh-mAN

I already have plans for Tuesday
j'ai déjà quelque chose de prévu mardi
zhay day-zha kel-kuh shohz duh pray-vU mar-dee

Understanding

une/deux fois
once/twice

trois fois par heure/jour
three times an hour/a day

tous les jours/lundis
every day/Monday

ça a été construit au milieu du dix-neuvième siècle
it was built in the mid-nineteenth century

il y a beaucoup de monde ici en été
it gets very busy here in the summer

vous êtes arrivé quand ?
when did you get here?

vous êtes ici pour combien temps ?
how long are you staying?

quand est-ce que vous partez ?
when are you leaving?

THE TIME

The twenty-four hour clock is commonly used in France, so you will hear people say **il est quatorze heures** for "it's 2 o'clock" (in the afternoon).

However, it is also acceptable to use the twelve-hour clock, if necessary adding **du matin** (in the morning, used until midday), **de l'après-midi** (in the afternoon, used until 5pm) or **du soir** (in the evening/at night, used for the rest of the evening).

The basics

early	tôt *toh*
half an hour	une demi-heure *Un duh-mee uhr*
in the afternoon	de l'après-midi *duh la-pray-mee-dee*
in the morning	du matin *dU ma-tAN*
late	tard *tar*
midday	midi *mee-dee*
midnight	minuit *meen-wee*
on time	à l'heure *a luhr*
quarter of an hour	quart d'heure *kar duhr*
three quarters of an hour	trois quarts d'heure *trwa kar duhr*

Expressing yourself

what time is it?
quelle heure est-il ?
kel uhr ay-teel ?

it's exactly three o'clock
il est trois/quinze heures pile
eel ay trwaz/kANz uhr peel

excuse me, have you got the time, please?
excusez-moi, est-ce que vous auriez l'heure ?
eks-kU-zay-mwa, ess kuh vooz oh-ryay luhr ?

it's nearly one o'clock
il est presque une heure/presque treize heures
eel ay presk Un uhr/preskuh trez uhr

it's twenty past twelve
il est midi vingt
eel ay mee-dee vAN

it's ten past one
il est une heure/treize heures dix
eel ay Un uhr/trez uhr dees

it's a quarter past one
il est une heure et quart/treize heures quinze
eel ay Un uhr ay kar/trez uhr kANz

it's a quarter to one
il est une heure moins le quart/douze heures quarante-cinq
eel ay Un uhr mwAN luh kar/dooz uhr ka-rONt-sANk

it's twenty to twelve
il est midi moins vingt
eel ay mee-dee mwAN vAN

it's half past one
il est une heure et demie/treize heures trente
eel ay Un uhr ay duh-mee/trez uhr trONt

I arrived at about two o'clock
je suis arrivé vers deux heures
zhuh sweez a-ree-vay ver duhz uhr

I set my alarm for nine
j'ai mis mon réveil à neuf heures
zhay mee mON ray-vey a nuhv uhr

I waited twenty minutes
j'ai attendu vingt minutes
zhay a-tON-dU vAN mee-nUt

the train was fifteen minutes late
le train a eu quinze minutes de retard
le trAN a U kANz mee-nUt duh ruh-tar

I got home an hour ago
je suis arrivé à la maison il y a une heure
zhuh sweez a-ree-vay a la may-zON eel ya Un uhr

shall we meet in half an hour?
on se retrouve dans une demi-heure ?
ON suh ruh-troov dONz Un duh-mee uhr ?

I'll be back in a quarter of an hour
je serai de retour dans un quart d'heure
zhuh suh-ray duh ruh-toor dONz AN kar duhr

there's a one-hour time difference between ... and ...
il y a une heure de décalage entre ... et ...
eel ya Un uhr duh day-ka-lazh ONtr ... ay ...

Understanding

ouvert de 10h à 19h	open from 10am to 7pm

ça joue tous les soirs à 20h
it's on every evening at eight

ça dure environ une heure et demie
it lasts around an hour and a half

ça ouvre à 10h
it opens at ten in the morning

Some informal expressions

à deux heures pile at two o'clock on the dot
être à la bourre to be late, to be in a big rush
grouille-toi ! get a move on!

NUMBERS

0 zéro *zay-roh*
1 un *AN*
2 deux *duh*
3 trois *trwa*
4 quatre *katr*
5 cinq *sANk*
6 six *sees*
7 sept *set*
8 huit *weet*
9 neuf *nuhf*
10 dix *dees*
11 onze *ONz*
12 douze *dooz*
13 treize *trez*
14 quatorze *ka-torz*
15 quinze *kANz*
16 seize *sez*
17 dix-sept *dees-set*
18 dix-huit *deez-weet*
19 dix-neuf *deez-nuhf*
20 vingt *vAN*
21 vingt et un *vAN-tay-AN*
22 vingt-deux *vANt-duh*
30 trente *trONt*
35 trente-cinq *trONt-sANk*

40 quarante *ka-rONt*
50 cinquante *sAN-kONt*
60 soixante *swa-sONt*
70 soixante-dix *swa-sONt-dees*
80 quatre-vingts *ka-truh-vAN*
90 quatre-vingt-dix *ka-truh-vAN-dees*
100 cent *sON*
101 cent un *sON-AN*
200 deux cents *duh sON*
500 cinq cents *sANk sON*
1000 mille *meel*
2000 deux mille *duh meel*
10 000 dix mille *dee meel*
1 000 000 un million *AN meel-yON*

first premier *pruhm-yay*
second deuxième *duhz-yem*
third troisième *trwaz-yem*
fourth quatrième *ka-tree-yem*
fifth cinquième *sANk-yem*
sixth sixième *seez-yem*
seventh septième *set-yem*
eighth huitième *weet-yem*
ninth neuvième *nuhv-yem*
tenth dixième *deez-yem*
twentieth vingtième *vANt-yem*

NUMBERS

20 plus 3 equals 23
vingt plus trois égale vingt-trois
vAN plUs trwa ay-gal vANt-trwa

20 minus 3 equals 17
vingt moins trois égale dix-sept
vAN mwAN trwa ay-gal dees-set

20 multiplied by 4 equals 80
vingt multiplié par quatre égale quatre-vingts
vAN mUl-tee-plee-yay par katr ay-gal ka-truh-vAN

20 divided by 4 equals 5
vingt divisé par quatre égale cinq
vAN dee-vee-zay par katr ay-gal sANk

DICTIONARY

ENGLISH-FRENCH

A

a un(e) *(see grammar)*
abbey abbaye *f*
able: to be able to pouvoir
about environ; **to be about to do** être sur le point de faire
above au-dessus (de), dessus
abroad à l'étranger
accept accepter
access accès *m* **114**
accident accident *m* **30, 113**
accommodation logement *mf*
across à travers
adaptor adaptateur *m*
address adresse *f* **18**
addressee destinataire *mf*
admission entrée *f* **70**
advance: in advance à l'avance **64**
advice conseils *mpl*; **to ask somebody's advice** demander conseil à quelqu'un
advise conseiller
affordable abordable
Africa Afrique *f*
after après
afternoon après-midi *m or f*
after-sun lait *m* après-soleil
again encore, à nouveau
against contre
age âge *m*
air air *m*
airbed matelas *m* pneumatique
air conditioning climatisation *f*
airline compagnie *f* aérienne
airmail par avion

airport aéroport *m*
airport tax taxe *f* d'aéroport
alarm clock réveil *m*
alcohol alcool *m*
alive vivant(e)
all tout(e); **all day/week** toute la journée/semaine; **all inclusive** tout compris; **all the better** tant mieux; **all the same** quand même; **all the time** tout le temps
allergic allergique **109**
almost presque
already déjà
also aussi
although quoique, bien que
always toujours
ambulance ambulance *f* **107**
American *(n)* Américain(e) *m,f; (adj)* américain(e)
among parmi
anaesthetic anesthésie *f*
and et
animal animal *m*
ankle cheville *f*
anniversary anniversaire *m*
another un(e) autre
answer *(n)* réponse *f; (v)* répondre
answering machine répondeur *m*
ant fourmi *f*
antibiotic antibiotique *m*
anybody, anyone n'importe qui
anything n'importe quoi
anyway de toute façon, bref
appendicitis appendicite *f*
appointment rendez-vous *m* **107**; **to make an appointment**

prendre un rendez-vous; **to have an appointment (with)** avoir rendez-vous (avec)

April avril m

area (of town) quartier m; (of country) région f; **in the area** dans la région

arm bras m

around (approximately) à peu près, vers

arrange arranger; **to arrange to meet** se donner rendez-vous

arrival arrivée f

arrive arriver

art art m

art gallery galerie f (d'art)

artist artiste mf

as comme; **as soon as possible** le plus tôt possible; **as soon as** dès que; **as well as** aussi bien que

ashamed: to be ashamed avoir honte

ashtray cendrier m **43**

Asia Asie f

ask demander; **to ask a question** poser une question

aspirin aspirine f

asthma asthme m

at à

attack (v) attaquer, agresser **113**

auditorium salle f de cinéma

August août m

autumn automne m

available libre, disponible

avenue avenue f

away: 2 km away à 2 km

ß

baby bébé m

baby's bottle biberon m

babysitter baby-sitter mf

back dos m; **at the back of** au fond de; **to be back** être de retour

backpack sac m à dos

bad mauvais; mal

bag sac m

baggage bagages mpl

baggage reclaim retrait m des bagages

bake cuire (au four)

baker's boulangerie f

balcony balcon m

ball (large) ballon m, (small) balle f

bandage bandage m

bank banque f **92**

bank account compte m bancaire

banknote billet m

bar bar m

barbecue barbecue m

bath bain m; **to have a bath** prendre un bain

bathroom salle f de bains

battery batterie f, pile f

be être

beach plage f

beach umbrella parasol m

beard barbe f

beautiful beau m, belle f

bed lit m; **to go to bed** aller se coucher, aller au lit

bed and breakfast chambres fpl d'hôte

bee abeille f

before avant; **before doing...** avant de faire...

begin commencer

beginner débutant(e) m,f

beginning début m; **at the beginning** au début

behind derrière

Belgian (n) Belge mf; (adj) belge

Belgium Belgique f

believe croire

below en dessous (de)

beside à côté de

best meilleur(e) m,f; **the best** le meilleur m, la meilleure f; **best wishes** meilleurs vœux; **all the best!** bonne continuation!

better (adj) meilleur(e); **better than...** meilleur(e) que...

better (adv) mieux; **better than…** mieux que…; **to get better** s'améliorer; guérir; **it's better to…** il vaut mieux…

between entre

bicycle bicyclette f

bicycle pump pompe f à vélo

big grand(e), gros m, grosse f

bike vélo m

bill facture f; (in restaurant) addition f, note f **48**

bin poubelle f

binoculars jumelles fpl

birthday anniversaire m

bit bout m, morceau m

bite (n) morsure f; (v) mordre

black (adj) noir(e); (n) noir m; **black and white** noir et blanc

blanket couverture f

bleed saigner

bless: bless you! à tes/vos souhaits!

blind aveugle

blister ampoule f

blond blond

blonde blonde

blood sang m

blood pressure tension f

blue (adj) bleu(e); (n) bleu m

board embarquer **25**

boarding embarquement m

boat bateau m

body corps m

book (n) livre m; **book of tickets** carnet m de tickets

book (v) réserver **31**

bookshop librairie m

boot (footwear) botte f; (of car) coffre m

borrow emprunter

boss patron m, patronne f, chef m

botanical garden jardin m botanique

both tous les deux m, toutes les deux f

bottle bouteille f; (baby's) biberon m

bottle opener décapsuleur m, ouvre-bouteilles m

bottom fond m; (buttocks) fesses fpl; **at the bottom** en bas; **at the bottom of** au fond de

bowl bol m

boxer shorts caleçon m

boy garçon m

boyfriend petit ami m, (informal) (petit) copain m

bra soutien-gorge m

brake (n) frein m; (v) freiner

bread pain m

break casser; **to break one's leg** se casser la jambe

break down tomber en panne **30**, **113**

breakdown panne f

breakdown service service m de dépannage

breakfast petit déjeuner m **36**; **to have breakfast** prendre le petit déjeuner

bridge pont m

bring apporter, amener

brochure brochure f

broken cassé(e)

bronchitis bronchite f

brother frère m

brown (adj) marron; (n) marron m

brush brosse f

build construire

building bâtiment m

bump bosse f

bumper pare-chocs m

buoy bouée f

burn (n) brûlure f

burn (v) brûler; **to burn oneself** se brûler

burst (v) crever; (adj) crevé(e)

bus autobus m, bus m **28**

bus route ligne f de bus

bus stop arrêt m de bus

business affaires fpl; **on business** pour affaires

business card carte f de visite

business class classe f affaires

business trip voyage m d'affaires

busy occupé(e), animé(e)
but mais
butcher's boucherie f
buy acheter **82**, **84**
by par; **by car** en voiture; **by the way…** au fait,…
bye! au revoir !, *(informal)* salut !

C

café café m
call *(n)* appel m; *(v)* appeler **103**
call back rappeler
camera appareil m photo; *(video)* caméra f
camper camping-car m
camping camping m; **to go camping** faire du camping **40**
camping stove camping-gaz® m
campsite (terrain m de) camping m
can *(n)* boîte f (de conserve)
can *(v)* pouvoir; **can you swim?** est-ce que tu sais nager?; **I can't** je ne peux pas
can opener ouvre-boîtes m
cancel annuler
candle bougie f
car voiture f; **by car** en voiture
caravan caravane f
card carte f
car park parking m
carry porter
case: in case of… en cas de…
cash liquide m; **to pay cash** payer en liquide
cashpoint distributeur m (automatique de billets) **92**
castle château m
catch attraper
cathedral cathédrale f
cavity: to have a cavity avoir une carie
CD CD m
cemetery cimetière m

centimetre centimètre m
centre centre m **36**
century siècle m
chair chaise f
chairlift télésiège m
chance hasard m; **by chance** par hasard
change *(n)* changement m; monnaie f **82, 83**; *(v)* changer **92**
changing room cabine f d'essayage **86**
channel *(TV)* chaîne f; **the (English) Channel** la Manche
chapel chapelle f
charge *(money)* faire payer; *(battery)* recharger
cheap bon marché
check *(v)* vérifier
check in enregistrer
check-in enregistrement m **25**
checkout caisse f
cheers! *(when drinking)* santé!; *(thanks)* merci!
chemist's pharmacie f'
cheque chèque m
chest poitrine f
child enfant mf
chilly frais m, fraîche f, froid(e)
chimney cheminée f
chin menton m
Chinese *(n)* Chinois(e) m,f; *(language)* chinois m; *(adj)* chinois(e)
Christmas Noël m
church *(Catholic)* église f; *(Protestant)* temple m
cigar cigare m
cigarette cigarette f
cigarette paper papier m à cigarette
cinema cinéma m
circus cirque m
city ville f
class *(lesson)* cours m; *(groupe)* classe f
classic classique
classical classique
clean *(adj)* propre

clean (v) nettoyer; **to clean one's teeth** se laver les dents
clementine clémentine f
cliff falaise f
climate climat m
climbing escalade f
cloakroom vestiaire m
close (v) fermer
closed fermé
closing fermeture f; **closing time** heure f de fermeture
clothes vêtements mpl
clutch embrayage m
coach (bus) autocar m, car m **28**; (of train) voiture f
coach station gare f routière
coast côte f
coathanger cintre m
cockroach cafard m
code code m
coffee café m
coil stérilet m
coin pièce f
Coke® Coca® m
cold (n) rhume m; **to have a cold** être enrhumé(e)
cold (adj) froid(e); **it's cold** il fait froid; **I'm cold** j'ai froid
collection (of objects) collection f; (postal) levée f
colour couleur f
comb peigne m
come venir
come back revenir
come in entrer
come out sortir
comfortable à l'aise, confortable
comic strip bande f dessinée
company société f
compartment compartiment m
complain se plaindre
comprehensive insurance assurance f tous risques
computer ordinateur m

concert concert m **65**
concert hall salle f de concert
concession tarif m réduit **23**, **71**
condom préservatif m
conference conférence f
confirm confirmer **25**
congratulations! félicitations !
connection lien m; (trains, planes) correspondance f **25**
constipated constipé(e)
consulate consulat m **113**
contact (n) contact m; (v) contacter
contact lenses lentilles fpl (de contact)
contagious contagieux m, contagieuse f
contemporary contemporain(e)
contraceptive contraceptif m
cook (v) cuisiner; (a dish) (faire) cuire
cook (n) cuisinier m, cuisinière f
cooked cuit(e)
cooking cuisine f; **to do the cooking** faire la cuisine
cool frais m, fraîche f; (trendy) branché(e)
corkscrew tire-bouchon m
corn maïs m
correct correct(e)
cost coûter
cotton coton m
cotton bud coton-tige® m
cotton wool coton m
couchette couchette f
cough (n) toux f; **to have a cough** avoir de la toux
cough (v) tousser
count compter
count on compter sur
country pays m; (countryside) campagne f
countryside campagne f
course: of course bien sûr
cover (n) couverture f; (v) couvrir
credit card carte f de crédit **35**, **48**
crisis crise f
cross (n) croix f; (v) traverser
cruise croisière f

cry *(v)* pleurer
culture culture *f*
cup tasse *f* **47**
currency devise *f*
customs douane *f*
cut couper; **to cut oneself** se couper
cycle path piste *f* cyclable **77**

D

damaged abîmé(e)
damp humide
dance *(n)* danse *f*; *(v)* danser
dangerous dangereux *m*, dangereuse *f*
dark foncé(e); **dark blue** bleu foncé;
  in the dark dans le noir
date *(n)* date *f*; rendez-vous *m*; **out
  of date** périmé(e); **what's today's
  date?** on est le combien?
date (from) *(v)* dater (de)
date of birth date *f* de naissance
daughter fille *f*
daughter-in-law belle-fille *f*
day jour *m*, journée *f*; **the day after
  tomorrow** après-demain; **the day
  before yesterday** avant-hier
dead mort(e)
deaf sourd(e)
dear cher *m*, chère *f*
debit card carte *f* bancaire
December décembre *m*
declare déclarer
deep profond(e)
degree degré *m*
delay retard *m*
delayed retardé(e)
deli épicerie *f* fine
dentist dentiste *mf*
deodorant déodorant *m*
department rayon *m*
department store grand magasin *m*
departure départ *m*
depend: it depends (on) ça dépend (de)
deposit caution *f*

desert désert *m*
deckchair transat *m*
dessert dessert *m* **45**
develop: to get a film developed
  faire développer une pellicule
diabetes diabète *m*
dialling code indicatif *m*
diarrhoea: to have diarrhoea avoir
  la diarrhée
dice dé *m*
die mourir
diesel diesel *m*
diet régime *m*; **to be on a diet** être
  au régime
different (from) différent(e) (de)
difficult (to) difficile (à)
dinner dîner *m*; **to have dinner** dîner
direct direct(e)
direction direction *f*, sens *m*; **to have
  a good sense of direction** avoir le
  sens de l'orientation
directory annuaire *m*
directory enquiries les
  renseignements *mpl*
dirty *(adj)* sale; **to get dirty** se salir
disabled handicapé(e) **114**
disappointed déçu(e)
disappointing décevant(e)
disaster catastrophe *f*
discount rabais *m* **70**; **to give
  somebody a discount** faire un rabais
  à quelqu'un
discount fare tarif *m* réduit
dish plat *m*
dishes vaisselle *f*; **to do the dishes**
  faire la vaisselle
dish towel torchon *m*
dishwasher lave-vaisselle *m*
disinfect désinfecter
disposable jetable
disturb déranger
dive plonger
diving plongée *f*; **to go diving** faire de
  la plongée

do faire; **do you have a light?** tu as du feu?

doctor médecin *m*, docteur *m* **106**, **107**

door porte *f*

door code code *m* d'entrée

downstairs en bas

draught beer pression *f*

dream *(n)* rêve *m*; *(v)* rêver

dress *(n)* robe *f*

dress: *(v)* **to get dressed** s'habiller

dressing pansement *m*

drink *(n)* boisson *f*; **to go for a drink** aller prendre un verre **43**, **66**; **to have a drink** prendre un verre

drink *(v)* boire

drinking water eau *f* potable

drive: *(n)* **to go for a drive** faire un tour (en voiture)

drive *(v)* conduire

driving licence permis *m* de conduire

drops gouttes *fpl*

drown se noyer

drug drogue *f*

drunk soûl(e)

dry *(adj)* sec *m*, sèche *f*; *(v)* (faire) sécher

dry cleaner's pressing *m*

duck canard *m*

during pendant; **during the week** en semaine

dustbin poubelle *f*

Dutch *(n)* Hollandais(e) *m,f*; *(language)* hollandais *m*; *(adj)* hollandais(e)

duty chemist's pharmacie *f* de garde

E

each chaque; **each one** chacun

ear oreille *f*

early en avance, tôt

earplugs boules *fpl* Quiès®

earrings boucles *fpl* d'oreilles

earth terre *f*

Earth la Terre

east est *m*; **in the east** à l'est; **(to the) east of** à l'est de

Easter Pâques

easy (to) facile (à)

eat manger **43**

economy class classe *f* économique

egg œuf *m*

Elastoplast® pansement *m*

electric électrique

electric shaver rasoir *m* électrique

electricity électricité *f*

electricity meter compteur *m* électrique

e-mail e-mail *m* **98**

e-mail address adresse *f* e-mail **18**, **98**

embassy ambassade *f*

emergency urgence *f*; **in an emergency** en cas d'urgence

emergency exit sortie *f* de secours

empty vide

end fin *f*; **at the end of** à la fin de; **at the end of the street** au bout de la rue

engaged occupé(e); **to be engaged** *(couple)* être fiancés

engine moteur *m*

England Angleterre *f*

English *(n)* Anglais(e) *m,f*; *(language)* anglais *m*; *(adj)* anglais(e)

enjoy: enjoy your meal! bon appétit!; **to enjoy oneself** bien s'amuser

enough assez (de); **that's enough** ça suffit

entrance entrée *f*

envelope enveloppe *f*

epileptic épileptique

equipment matériel *m*

espresso express *m*

euro euro *m*

Eurocheque eurochèque *m*

Europe Europe *f*

European *(n)* Européen(ne) *m,f*; *(adj)* européen *m*, européenne *f*

European Union Union *f* européenne

evening soir m, soirée f; **in the evening** dans la soirée; **in the evenings** le soir
every tout(e); **every day** tous les jours
everybody, everyone tout le monde
everywhere partout
except sauf
exceptional exceptionnel m, exceptionnelle f
excess excès m; **excess baggage** excédent m de bagages
exchange échanger
exchange rate taux m de change
excuse (n) excuse f
excuse: (v) **excuse me** pardon, excusez-moi
exhausted épuisé(e)
exhaust pipe pot m d'échappement
exhibition exposition f **70**
exit sortie f
expensive cher m, chère f
expiry date date f d'expiration
express (v) exprimer; **to express oneself** s'exprimer
expresso express m
extra supplémentaire
eye œil m

F

face (n) visage m
facecloth gant m de toilette
fact fait m; **in fact** en fait
faint s'évanouir
fair (n) foire f
fair (adj) juste
fall (v) tomber; **to fall asleep** s'endormir; **to fall ill** tomber malade; **to fall in love (with)** tomber amoureux (de)
family famille f
famous célèbre
fan ventilateur m
far loin; **far from** loin de
fare tarif m

fast vite
fast-food restaurant fast-food m
fat (adj) gras m, grasse f
father père m
favour service m; **to do somebody a favour** rendre un service à quelqu'un; **to be in favour of something** être pour quelque chose
favourite préféré(e)
fax fax m
February février m
fed up: to be fed up (with) en avoir marre (de)
feel (se) sentir **107**; **to feel good/bad** se sentir bien/mal
feeling sentiment m
ferry ferry m
festival festival m
fetch: to go and fetch somebody/ something aller chercher quelqu'un/ quelque chose
fever fièvre f
few peu (de)
fiancé fiancé m
fiancée fiancée f
fight bagarre f
fill remplir
fill in/out remplir
fill up: to fill up with petrol faire le plein (d'essence)
filling plombage m
film film m; (for camera) pellicule f **89**
finally enfin, finalement
find trouver
fine (n) amende f
fine (adj) fin(e); **I'm fine** ça va
finger doigt m
finish finir
fire feu m, incendie m; **fire!** au feu !
fire brigade pompiers mpl
fireplace cheminée f
fireworks feux mpl d'artifice
first premier m, première f; **first (of all)** d'abord

first class première classe f
first name prénom m
fish (n) poisson m; (v) pêcher
fishmonger's poissonnerie f
fitting room cabine f d'essayage
fizzy gazeux m, gazeuse f
flash flash m
flask gourde f
flat (adj) plat(e); (tyre) dégonflé(e)
flat (n) appartement m
flavour parfum m
flaw défaut m
flight vol m
flip-flops tongs fpl
floor (of building) étage m; (ground) sol
   m; **on the floor** par terre
floppy (disk) disquette f
flu grippe f
flush chasse f d'eau
fly (n) mouche f
fly (v) voler
food nourriture f
food poisoning intoxication f
   alimentaire
foot pied m
for pour; **for an hour** pendant une
   heure
forbidden interdit(e)
forecast (v) prévoir
forehead front m
foreign étranger m, étrangère f
foreigner étranger m, étrangère f
forest forêt f
fork fourchette f
former ancien m, ancienne f
forward (v) faire suivre
forward (adj) avant; **forward gear**
   marche avant
four-star petrol super m
fracture fracture f
fragile fragile
France France f
free gratuit(e) **69**; libre
freezer congélateur m

French (n) Français(e) m,f; (language)
   français m; (adj) français(e)
Friday vendredi m
fridge frigo m
fried frit(e); **fried egg** œuf m sur le plat
friend ami(e) m,f, (informal) copain m,
   copine f
fries frites fpl
from (à partir) de; **from ... to ...** de
   ... à ...
front avant; **in front of** devant
front wheel roue f avant
frozen food surgelés mpl
fruit fruits mpl
fruit juice jus m de fruit
fry (faire) frire
frying pan poêle f
full plein(e); (hotel etc) complet m,
   complète f; **full of** plein(e) de
full board pension f complète
full fare, full price plein tarif m
funfair fête f foraine
fuse fusible m

G

game jeu m; (meat) gibier m
garage garage m **30**
garden jardin m
gas gaz m
gas cylinder bouteille f de gaz
gastric flu grippe f intestinale
gate barrière f; (in airport) porte f
gauze gaze f
gearbox boîte f de vitesses
gel gel m
general général(e)
gents' (toilet) toilettes fpl pour
   hommes
German (n) Allemand(e) m,f; (language)
   allemand m; (adj) allemand(e)
Germany Allemagne f
get obtenir; (receive) recevoir
get off descendre **28**

get on: to get on well (with someone) bien s'entendre (avec quelqu'un)
get up se lever
gift wrap papier *m* cadeau
girl fille *f*
girlfriend petite amie *f*, *(informal)* (petite) copine *f*
give donner; **to give somebody a present** offrir un cadeau à quelqu'un
give back rendre
glass verre *m*; **a glass of water/of wine** un verre d'eau/de vin
glasses lunettes *fpl*
go aller; **to go to Paris/to France** aller à Paris/en France; **I'm going home** je rentre chez moi
go away s'en aller
go in entrer
go out sortir; **to go out with someone** sortir avec quelqu'un
go with aller avec; *(accompany)* accompagner
go without se passer de
golf golf *m*
golf course terrain *m* de golf
good bon *m*, bonne *f*; bien; **good luck!** bon courage !, bonne chance !; **good morning** bonjour; **good afternoon** bonjour; **good evening** bonsoir
goodbye au revoir
goodnight bonne nuit
goods marchandises *fpl*
Gothic gothique
GP généraliste *mf*
grams grammes *mpl*
grass herbe *f*
great super
Great Britain Grande-Bretagne *f*
Greece Grèce *f*
Greek *(n)* Grec *m*, Grecque *f*; *(language)* grec *m*; *(adj)* grec *m*, grecque *f*
green *(adj)* vert *m*, verte *f*; *(n)* vert *m*

grey *(adj)* gris(e); *(n)* gris *m*
grocer's épicerie *f*
ground sol *m*; **on the ground** par terre
ground floor rez-de-chaussée *m*
groundsheet tapis *m* de sol
grow grandir; *(cultivate)* cultiver
guarantee garantie *f*
guest invité(e) *m,f*
guest house chambre *f* d'hôtes
guide guide *mf* **64**
guidebook guide *m*
guided tour visite *f* guidée
gynaecologist gynécologue *mf*

H

hair cheveux *mpl*
hairdresser coiffeur *m*, coiffeuse *f*
hairdrier sèche-cheveux *m*
half *(adj)* demi; *(n)* moitié *f*; **half a litre/kilo** un demi-litre/-kilo; **half an hour** une demi-heure
half-board demi-pension *f*
half-pint: a half-pint un demi
hand main *f*
handbag sac *m* à main
handbrake frein *m* à main
handkerchief mouchoir *m*
hand luggage bagages *mpl* à main **25**
handmade fait(e) main
hangover gueule *f* de bois
happen arriver, se passer
happy heureux *m*, heureuse *f*; **happy birthday!** bon anniversaire !; **Happy Easter!** joyeuses Pâques !; **Happy New Year!** bonne année !
hard dur(e)
hard disk disque *m* dur
hat chapeau *m*
hate détester
have avoir; **to have a headache/a sore throat/a sore stomach** avoir mal à la tête/à la gorge/au ventre; **to have to** devoir

hay fever rhume *m* des foins
he il
head tête *f*
headlight phare *m*
health santé *f*
hear entendre
heart cœur *m*
heart attack crise *f* cardiaque
heat chaleur *f*
heating chauffage *m*
heavy lourd(e)
hello bonjour; *(in evening)* bonsoir; *(on telephone)* allô
helmet casque *m*
help *(n)* aide *f*, secours *m*; **to call for help** appeler au secours; **help!** au secours !
help *(v)* aider **112**
her la; lui; son, sa, ses *(see grammar)*
herbal tea tisane *f*
here ici; **here is/are** voici
hers le sien, la sienne, les siens/siennes *(see grammar)*
hi! bonjour !, *(informal)* salut !
hi-fi chaîne *f* (hi-fi)
high haut(e)
high blood pressure hypertension *f*
high heels chaussures *fpl* à talons
high tide marée *f* haute
hiking randonnée *f*; **to go hiking** faire de la randonnée
hill colline *f*
hill-walking randonnée *f* **75**; **to go hill-walking** faire de la randonnée
him le; lui *(see grammar)*
himself lui-même
hip hanche *f*
hire *(n)* location *f*; *(v)* louer **30**, **74**, **77**
his son, sa, ses; le sien, la sienne, les siens/siennes *(see grammar)*
hitchhike faire du stop
hitchhiking stop *m*
hold tenir; **hold on** *(on the phone)* ne quittez pas

holiday(s) vacances *fpl*; **on holiday** en vacances **17**
holiday camp colonie *f* de vacances
Holland Hollande *f*
home maison *f*; **at home** à la maison, chez soi; **to go home** rentrer
homosexual homosexuel *m*, homosexuelle *f*
honest honnête
honeymoon lune *f* de miel
horse cheval *m*
hospital hôpital *m*
hot chaud(e); **it's hot today** il fait chaud aujourd'hui; **hot drinks** boissons *fpl* chaudes
hot chocolate chocolat *m* chaud
hotel hôtel *m*
hotplate plaque *f* électrique
hour heure *f*; **an hour and a half** une heure et demie
house maison *f*
housework ménage *m*; **to do the housework** faire le ménage
how comment; **how are you?** comment allez-vous ?, ça va ?
humour humour *m*; **to have a good sense of humour** avoir le sens de l'humour
hunger faim *f*
hungry: to be hungry avoir faim **43**
hurry: *(n)* **to be in a hurry** être pressé
hurry (up) se dépêcher
hurt: it hurts ça fait mal; **my head hurts** j'ai mal à la tête
husband mari *m*

I

I je; **I'm French** je suis Français(e); **I'm 22 (years old)** j'ai 22 ans
ice glace *f*
ice cream glace *f*
ice cube glaçon *m*

identity card carte *f* d'identité

if si; **if ever** si jamais

ill malade

illness maladie *f*

important important(e)

in dans; en; **in France/2006/English** en France/2006/anglais; **in the 19th century** au XIXᵉ siècle; **in an hour** dans une heure

included compris(e)

independent indépendant(e)

indicator clignotant *m*

infection infection *f*

information renseignements *mpl*, informations *fpl* **69**

injection piqûre *f*

injured blessé(e)

inner tube chambre *f* à air

insect insecte *m*

insecticide insecticide *m*

inside à l'intérieur (de), dedans

insomnia insomnie *f*

instant coffee Nescafé® *m*

instead of au lieu de

insurance assurance *f*

intend to... avoir l'intention de...

intermission entracte *m*

international international(e)

international money order mandat *m* international

Internet Internet *m*

Internet café café *m* Internet, cybercafé *m* **98**

interval entracte *m*

invite inviter

iron (*n*) fer *m* à repasser; (*v*) repasser

island île *f*

it ce; il, elle; le, la, lui (*see grammar*); **it's beautiful** c'est beau; **it's warm** il fait chaud

Italian (*n*) Italien *m*, Italienne *f*; (*language*) italien *m*; (*adj*) italien *m*, italienne *f*

Italy Italie *f*

itchy: it's itchy ça me démange

item article *m*

jacket veste *f*; (*bomber jacket*) blouson *m*

January janvier *m*

Japan Japon *m*

Japanese (*n*) Japonais(e) *m,f*; (*language*) japonais *m*; (*adj*) japonais(e)

jetlag décalage *m* horaire

jeweller's bijouterie *f*

jewellery bijoux *mpl*

job travail *m*, (*informal*) boulot *m*

jogging jogging *m*

journey voyage *m*

jug carafe *f*

juice jus *m*

July juillet *m*

jumper pull *m*

June juin *m*

just: just before/a little juste avant/un peu; **just one** un seul; **I've just arrived** je viens d'arriver; **just in case** au cas où

kayak kayak *m*

keep garder

key clé *f* **30**, **37**, **39**

kidney rein *m*; (*food*) rognon *m*

kill tuer

kilometre kilomètre *m*

kind: what kind of ...? quel genre de ... ?

kiss (*n*) bise *f*; (*v*) embrasser

kitchen cuisine *f*

Kleenex® Kleenex® *m*

knee genou *m*

knickers culotte *f*

knife couteau *m*

knock down/over renverser; **to get knocked down/over** se faire renverser

know connaître, savoir

L

ladies' (toilet) toilettes *fpl* pour femmes
lake lac *m*
lamp lampe *f*
landmark (point *m* de) repère *m*
landscape paysage *m*
language langue *f*
laptop (ordinateur *m*) portable *m*
last *(adj)* dernier *m*, dernière *f*; **last year** l'année dernière
last *(v)* durer
late tard; *(in arriving)* en retard **25**, **63**
late-night opening nocturne *f*
latte café *m* crème
laugh rire
launderette laverie *f*
lawyer avocat *m*
leaflet prospectus *m*, dépliant *m*
leak fuite *f*
learn apprendre
least: the least le/la moins; **at least** au moins
leave partir; laisser
left *(adj)* gauche; *(n)* gauche *f*; **to the left (of)** à gauche (de)
left-luggage office consigne *f*
leg jambe *f*
lend prêter
lens objectif *m*
lenses lentilles *fpl*
less moins; **less than** moins que
let laisser
letter lettre *f*
letterbox boîte *f* aux lettres
library bibliothèque *f*
lie down se coucher, s'étendre
life vie *f*
lift ascenseur *m*
light *(adj)* léger *m*, légère *f*; **light blue** bleu clair
light *(n)* lumière *f*

light *(v)* allumer
light bulb ampoule *f*
lighter briquet *m*
lighthouse phare *m*
like *(adv)* comme
like *(v)* aimer, aimer bien **19**; **I'd like …** j'aimerais …
lip lèvre *f*
listen écouter; **to listen to somebody/something** écouter quelqu'un/quelque chose
listings magazine guide *m* des spectacles
litre litre *m*
little *(adj)* petit(e)
little *(adv)* peu de; **a little** un peu; **little by little** petit à petit
live habiter, vivre
liver foie *m*
living vivant(e)
living room salon *m*
local time heure *f* locale
lock serrure *f*; *(bolt)* verrou *m*
lollipop sucette *f*
long long *m*, longue *f*; **a long time** longtemps; **how long …?** combien de temps … ?; **how long have you been here?** depuis quand êtes-vous ici ?
look regarder; **to look tired** avoir l'air fatigué
look after surveiller, s'occuper de
look at regarder
look for chercher
look like ressembler à
lorry camion *m*
lose perdre **30**, **113**; **to get lost** se perdre; **to be lost** être perdu **12**
lot: a lot (of) beaucoup (de)
loud fort(e)
low bas *m*, basse *f*
low blood pressure hypotension *f*
low tide marée *f* basse
luck chance *f*
lucky: to be lucky avoir de la chance

luggage bagages *mpl* **25**
lukewarm tiède
lunch déjeuner *m*; **to have lunch** déjeuner
lung poumon *m*
Luxembourg Luxembourg *m*
luxury *(n)* luxe *m*; *(adj)* de luxe

M

magazine magazine *m*, revue *f*
maiden name nom *m* de jeune fille
mail courrier *m*; *(e-mail)* e-mail *m*
main principal(e)
main course plat *m* principal
make faire; *(manufacture)* fabriquer
man homme *m*
manage se débrouiller; **to manage to do something** arriver à faire quelque chose
management direction *f*
many beaucoup (de); **how many?** combien?; **how many times …?** combien de fois … ?
map plan *m* **12**, **27**, **63**, **69**
March mars *m*
market marché *m* **84**
marina port *m* de plaisance
marriage mariage *m*
married marié(e)
mass messe *f*
masterpiece chef-d'œuvre *m*
match *(for lighting fire)* allumette *f*; *(game)* match *m*
material tissu *m*
matter: it doesn't matter ça ne fait rien
mattress matelas *m*
May mai *m*
maybe peut-être
me me; moi; **me too** moi aussi *(see grammar)*
meal repas *m*
mean vouloir dire, signifier

medicine médicament *m*
medium moyen *m*, moyenne *f*; *(steak)* à point
meet rencontrer; *(by arrangement)* rejoindre **63**
meeting réunion *f*
member membre *mf*
memory souvenir *m*; **in memory of** en souvenir de
men hommes *mpl*
menu carte *f*; *(set menu)* menu *m*
Merry Christmas! joyeux Noël !
message message *m* **102**
metre mètre *m*
microwave micro-ondes *m*
midday midi *m*
middle milieu *m*; **in the middle (of)** au milieu (de)
midnight minuit *m*
might: it might rain il risque de pleuvoir
mill moulin *m*
mind: I don't mind ça m'est égal
mine le mien, la mienne, les miens/ miennes *(see grammar)*
mineral water eau *f* minérale
minister ministre *mf*
minute minute *f*; **at the last minute** au dernier moment
mirror glace *f*
Miss Mademoiselle *f*
miss rater, manquer **25**; **I miss him** il me manque; **there are two … missing** il manque deux …
mistake erreur *f*, faute *f*; **to make a mistake** se tromper
mobile phone (téléphone *m*) portable *m* **113**
modern moderne
moisturizer crème *f* hydratante
moment moment *m*; **at the moment** en ce moment; **for the moment** pour le moment; **just a moment!** un moment !

monastery monastère *m*
Monday lundi *m*
money argent *m*
month mois *m*
monument monument *m*
mood: to be in a good/bad mood être de bonne/mauvaise humeur
moon lune *f*
moped Mobylette® *f*
more plus; **more than** plus que; **much more, a lot more** beaucoup plus; **there's no more room** il n'y a plus de place; **there are no more …** il n'y a plus de …
morning matin *m*
morning-after pill pilule *f* du lendemain
mosque mosquée *f*
mosquito moustique *m*
most: the most le/la plus; **most people** la plupart des gens; **to make the most of** profiter de
mother mère *f*
motorbike moto *f*
motorcycle moto *f*
motorway autoroute *f*
mountain montagne *f*
mountain bike VTT *m*
mouse souris *f*
mouth bouche *f*
moving émouvant(e)
Mr Monsieur *m*
Mrs Madame *f*
much: how much? combien ? **82**; **how much is it?, how much does it cost?** combien ça coûte ?
mug tasse *f*
muscle muscle *m*
museum musée *m*
music musique *f*
must devoir; **it must be 5 o'clock** il doit être 5 heures; **I must go** il faut que j'y aille
mustard moutarde *f*

my mon, ma, mes *(see grammar)*
myself moi-même

N

nail *(on finger, toe)* ongle *m*; *(for attaching)* clou *m*
naked nu(e)
name nom *m*; **my name is …** je m'appelle …
nap sieste *f*; **to have a nap** faire la sieste
napkin serviette *f* (de table)
nappy couche *f*
national holiday fête *f* nationale
nature nature *f*
near près; proche; **near the beach** près de la plage; **the nearest** le plus proche
necessary nécessaire
neck cou *m*
need avoir besoin de
negative négatif *m*
neighbour voisin(e) *m,f*
neither: neither do I moi non plus; **neither … nor …** ni … ni …
nephew neveu *m*
nervous nerveux *m*, nerveuse *f*
Netherlands Pays-Bas *mpl*
never ne … jamais
new nouveau *m*, nouvelle *f*; *(brand new)* neuf *m*, neuve *f*
news nouvelles *fpl*
newsagent marchand *m* de journaux
newspaper journal *m*
New Year nouvel an *m*
next *(adj)* prochain(e), suivant(e); *(adv)* ensuite
nice agréable; *(informal)* sympa
niece nièce *f*
night nuit *f* **35**, **38**
nightclub boîte *f* de nuit
nightdress chemise *f* de nuit
no non; aucun(e); **no, thank you** non merci; **no idea** aucune idée

nobody personne

noise bruit m; **to make a noise** faire du bruit

noisy bruyant(e)

none aucun(e)

non-smokers non-fumeurs mpl

noon midi m

north nord m; **in the north** au nord; **(to the) north of** au nord de

North Sea mer f du Nord

nose nez m

not ne … pas; **not yet** pas encore; **not any** aucun(e); **not at all** pas du tout

note mot m

notebook cahier m

nothing ne … rien

novel roman m

November novembre m

now maintenant

nowadays de nos jours

nowhere nulle part

number numéro m; (numeral) nombre m

nurse infirmière f

O

obvious évident(e)

occupation métier m

ocean océan m

o'clock: one o'clock une heure; **three o'clock** trois heures

October octobre m

of de

offer (v) offrir

often souvent

oil huile f

ointment pommade f

OK d'accord, (informal) ok

old vieux m, vieille f; (former) ancien m, ancienne f; **how old are you?** quel âge as-tu?; **old people** les personnes âgées fpl

old town vieille ville f

on sur; **it's on at …** ça joue à …

once une fois; **once a day/an hour** une fois par jour/heure

one (number) un; (personal pronoun) on

only ne … que, seulement

open (adj) ouvert(e); (v) ouvrir

operate opérer

operation: to have an operation se faire opérer

opinion avis m, opinion f; **in my opinion** à mon avis

opportunity occasion f

opposite (adj) contraire; (prep) en face de

optician opticien m

or ou

orange (adj) orange; (n) (fruit) orange f; (colour) orange m

orchestra orchestre m

order (n) commande f; (v) commander **45**

organic bio

organize organiser

other autre; **others** d'autres

otherwise sinon

our notre, nos (see grammar)

ours le/la nôtre, les nôtres (see grammar)

out of order hors service

outside dehors; (in the open air) en plein air

outward journey aller n

oven four m

over sur, au-dessus de; **over there** là-bas

overdone trop cuit(e)

owe devoir **48**

own (adj) propre; (v) posséder

owner propriétaire mf

P

pack: (v) **to pack one's bags** faire ses valises

package holiday voyage m organisé

packed bondé(e)

packet paquet m

painting peinture f, tableau m

pair paire f; **a pair of pyjamas/shorts** un pyjama m/short m

palace palais m

pants (woman's) culotte f, (man's) slip m

paper napkin serviette f en papier

parcel colis m

pardon? comment ?

parents parents mpl

park (n) parc m; (v) se garer

parking space place f de parking

part partie f; **to be a part of** faire partie de

party (for an occasion) fête f; (in the evening) soirée f

pass (n) forfait m

pass (v) passer; **to be passing through** être de passage

passenger passager m, passagère f

passport passeport m

past passé m; **a quarter past ten** dix heures et quart

path chemin m, sentier m **76**

patient patient(e)

pay payer **83**

pedestrian piéton m, piétonne f

pedestrian street rue f piétonne

pee: to have a pee faire pipi

peel peler

pen stylo m

pencil crayon m

people (les) gens mpl

percent pour cent

perfect parfait(e)

perfume parfum m

perhaps peut-être

periods règles fpl

person personne f

personal stereo Walkman® m

petrol essence f **29**

petrol station station-service f **29**

phone (n) téléphone m; (v) téléphoner (à)

phone box cabine f téléphonique **101**

phone call coup m de téléphone; **to make a phone call** passer un coup de téléphone

phonecard carte f de téléphone **101**

phone number numéro m de téléphone

photo photo f **88, 89**; **to take a photo/photos** prendre une photo/des photos; **to take somebody's photo** prendre quelqu'un en photo

photocopy photocopie f; **to make a photocopy** faire une photocopie

picnic pique-nique m; **to have a picnic** pique-niquer

piece morceau m; **a piece of** un morceau de; **a piece of advice/fruit** un conseil/fruit

piles hémorroïdes fpl

pill pilule f; **to be on the pill** prendre la pilule

pillow oreiller m

pillowcase taie f d'oreiller

PIN (number) code m confidentiel

pink (adj) rose; (n) (flower) rose f; (colour) rose m

pity: it's a pity c'est dommage

place lieu m

plan (v) prévoir

plane avion m **25**

plant plante f

plaster (cast) plâtre m

plastic plastique m

plastic bag sac m plastique

plate assiette f

platform quai m **27**

play (n) pièce f de théâtre; (v) jouer (à)

please (v) plaire; (adv) (informal) s'il te plaît, (polite or plural) s'il vous plaît

pleased content(e); **pleased to meet you!** enchanté(e) !

pleasure plaisir m

plug prise f

plug in brancher

plumber plombier *m*
point point *m*
police police *f*
policeman policier *m*
police station commissariat *m* **113**
poor pauvre
port port *m*
portrait portrait *m*
Portugal Portugal *m*
Portuguese *(n)* Portugais(e) *m,f;*
  (language) portugais *m; (adj)*
  portugais(e)
possible possible
post poste *f; (mail received)* courrier *m*
postbox boîte *f* aux lettres **95**
postcard carte *f* postale
postcode code *m* postal
poster affiche *f*
postman facteur *m*
post office bureau *m* de poste **94**
pot pot *m*
pound livre *f* (sterling); *(for cars)*
  fourrière *f*
powder poudre *f*
practical pratique
prefer préférer
pregnant enceinte **109**
prepare préparer
present cadeau *m*
press appuyer
pressure pression *f*
pretty joli(e), mignon *m*, mignonne *f*
previous précédent(e)
price prix *m*, tarif *m*
private privé(e)
prize prix *m*
probably probablement
problem problème *m*
product produit *m*
programme émission *f*, programme *m*
promise promettre
propose proposer
protect protéger; **to protect oneself**
  se protéger

proud fier *m*, fière *f*
public public *m*
public holiday jour *m* férié
pull tirer
purple *(adj)* violet *m*, violette *f; (n)*
  violet *m*
purpose: on purpose exprès
purse porte-monnaie *m*
push pousser
pushchair poussette *f*
put mettre
put out éteindre
put up héberger
put up with supporter

Q

quality qualité *f;* **of good/bad quality**
  de bonne/mauvaise qualité
quarter quart *m;* **a quarter of an**
  hour un quart d'heure; **a quarter to**
  ten dix heures moins le quart
quay quai *m*
question question *f*
queue *(n)* queue *f; (v)* faire la queue
quick rapide
quickly vite, rapidement
quiet calme, tranquille
quite assez de; **quite a lot of** pas
  mal de

R

racist raciste
racket raquette *f*
radiator radiateur *m*
radio radio *f*
radio station station *f* de radio
rain *(n)* pluie *f*
rain: *(v)* **it's raining** il pleut
raincoat imperméable *m*
random: at random au hasard
rape viol *m*
rare rare; *(meat)* saignant(e)

rarely rarement
rather plutôt
raw cru(e)
razor rasoir *m*
razor blade lame *f* de rasoir
reach arriver à
read lire
ready prêt(e)
reasonable raisonnable
receipt reçu *m*, ticket *m* de caisse **83**
receive recevoir
reception accueil *m*, réception *f*; **at reception** à la réception **38**
receptionist réceptionniste *mf*
recipe recette *f*
recognize reconnaître
recommend recommander **43**
record *(n)* disque *m*; *(v)* enregistrer
record dealer disquaire *m*
red *(adj)* rouge; *(hair)* roux *m*, rousse *f*; *(n)* rouge *m*
red light feu *m* rouge
reduce diminuer
reduction réduction *f*
red wine vin *m* rouge
refund *(n)* remboursement *m*; **to get a refund** se faire rembourser
refund *(v)* rembourser
refuse refuser
registered en recommandé
registration number numéro *m* d'immatriculation
remember se souvenir (de)
remind rappeler; **that reminds me of …** ça me rappelle …
remove enlever
rent *(n)* loyer *m*; *(v)* louer **39**; **for rent** à louer
rental location *f*
reopen rouvrir
repair réparer **30**; **to get something repaired** faire réparer quelque chose
repeat répéter **10**
reserve réserver **44**

reserved réservé(e)
rest: *(n)* **the rest** le reste
rest *(v)* se reposer
restaurant restaurant *m* **43**
return retour *m*
return ticket aller-retour *m*
reverse-charge call appel *m* en PCV **101**
reverse gear marche *f* arrière
review critique *f*
rheumatism rhumatismes *mpl*
rib côte *f*
right *(n)* *(entitlement)* droit *m*; *(side)* droite *f*; **to have the right to …** avoir le droit de …; **to the right (of)** à droite (de)
right *(adj)* bon *m*, bonne *f*; **to be right** avoir raison
right: *(adv)* **right away** tout de suite; **right beside** tout près de
ring bague *f*
ripe mûr(e)
rip-off arnaque *f*
risk risque *m*
river fleuve *m*, rivière *f*
road route *f*; *(street)* rue *f*
road sign panneau *m*
rock rocher *m*
rollerblades rollers *mpl*
room pièce *f*, salle *f*; *(bedroom)* chambre *f* **35**, **36**
rosé wine rosé *m*
round tournée *f*
roundabout rond-point *m*
rubbish ordures *fpl*; **to take the rubbish out** sortir les poubelles
rucksack sac *m* à dos
rug tapis *m*
ruins ruines *fpl*; **in ruins** en ruines
run out: to have run out of petrol être en panne d'essence **30**

sad triste
safe en sécurité
safety sécurité f
safety belt ceinture f de sécurité
sail voile f
sailing voile f; **to go sailing** faire de la voile
sailing boat bateau m à voile
sale: for sale à vendre; **in the sale** en solde
sales soldes fpl
salt sel m
salted salé(e)
salty salé(e)
same même, pareil m, pareille f; **the same** le même m, la même f, les mêmes mfpl
sand sable m
sandals sandales fpl
sanitary towel serviette f hygiénique
Saturday samedi m
saucepan casserole f
save sauver; (on computer) sauvegarder; **to save time** gagner du temps
say dire; **how do you say …?** comment dit-on … ?
scared: to be scared (of) avoir peur (de)
scenery paysage m
scissors ciseaux mpl
scoop (of ice cream) boule f
scooter scooter m
scotch whisky m
scuba diving plongée f sous-marine
sea mer f
seafood fruits mpl de mer
seasick: to be seasick avoir le mal de mer
seaside: at the seaside au bord de la mer
seaside resort station f balnéaire
season saison f

seat place f **23**
sea view vue f sur mer
seaweed algues fpl
second seconde f
second class deuxième classe f
secondary school collège m; (age 15-18) lycée m
second-hand d'occasion
secure en sécurité
security sécurité f
see voir; **see you later!** à plus tard !, à tout à l'heure !; **see you soon!** à bientôt !, à la prochaine !; **see you tomorrow!** à demain !
seem paraître; **it seems that …** il paraît que …
seldom pas souvent
self-confidence confiance f en soi
sell vendre
Sellotape® Scotch® m
send envoyer
sender expéditeur m
sense sens m
sensitive sensible
sentence phrase f
separate séparer
separately séparément
September septembre m
serious sérieux m, sérieuse f; (accident etc) grave
several plusieurs
sex sexe m
shade ombre f; **in the shade** à l'ombre
shame honte f
shampoo shampooing m
shape forme f
share partager
shave se raser
shaving cream crème f à raser
shaving foam mousse f à raser
she elle
sheet drap m; (of paper) feuille f
shellfish crustacés mpl

shirt chemise f
shock choc m
shocking choquant(e)
shoes chaussures fpl
shop magasin m
shop assistant vendeur m, vendeuse f
shopkeeper marchand(e) m,f
shopping courses fpl; (for clothes, presents) shopping m; **to do some/the shopping** faire des/les courses
shopping centre centre m commercial
short court(e); **I'm two ... short** il me manque deux …
short cut raccourci m
shorts short m
short-sleeved en/à manches courtes
shoulder épaule f
show (n) spectacle m; (v) montrer
shower douche f; **to take a shower** prendre une douche
shower gel gel m douche
shut fermer
shuttle navette f
shy timide
sick: to feel sick avoir mal au cœur
side côté m
sign (n) panneau m; (v) signer
sign up s'inscrire
signal réception f
silver argent m
since depuis (que); (because) puisque
sing chanter
singer chanteur m, chanteuse f
single célibataire mf
single (ticket) aller m (simple)
sister sœur f
sit down s'asseoir
size taille f; (of shoes) pointure f
ski ski m
ski boots chaussures fpl de ski
skiing ski m; **to go skiing** faire du ski
ski lift remontée f mécanique
ski pole bâton m de ski
ski resort station f de ski

skin peau f
skirt jupe f
sky ciel m
skyscraper gratte-ciel m
sleep (n) sommeil m
sleep (v) dormir; **to sleep with** coucher avec
sleeping bag sac m de couchage
sleeping pill somnifère m
sleepy: to be sleepy avoir sommeil
sleeve manche f
slice tranche f
sliced coupé(e) en tranches
slide diapositive f
slow lent(e)
slowly lentement, doucement
small petit(e); **smaller than** plus petit(e) que
smell (n) odeur f
smell (v) sentir; **to smell good/bad** sentir bon/mauvais
smile (n) sourire m; (v) sourire
smoke fumer
smoker fumeur m, fumeuse f
snack casse-croûte m
snow (n) neige f; (v) neiger
so si, alors; **so that** pour que
soap savon m
soccer football m
society société f
socks chaussettes fpl
some (adj) quelques; (pron) quelques-uns mpl, quelques-unes fpl
somebody, someone quelqu'un
something quelque chose; **something else** autre chose
sometimes quelquefois
somewhere quelque part; **somewhere else** ailleurs
son fils m
song chanson f
soon bientôt
sore: to have a sore throat/head avoir mal à la gorge/tête

sorry désolé(e); **sorry!** pardon !
south sud *m*; **in the south** au sud; **(to the) south of** au sud de
souvenir souvenir *m*
Spain Espagne *f*
Spanish *(n)* Espagnol(e) *m,f; (language)* espagnol *m; (adj)* espagnol(e)
spare ... ... de rechange
spare part pièce *f* de rechange
spare wheel roue *f* de secours
sparkling water eau *f* gazeuse
speak parler **8, 10, 102, 113**
special spécial(e); **it's nothing special** ça n'a rien d'exceptionnel; **today's special** plat *m* du jour **45**
speciality spécialité *f*
speed vitesse *f*; **at full speed** à toute vitesse
spell épeler **10**
spend dépenser; *(time)* passer
spice épice *f*
spicy épicé(e)
spider araignée *f*
splinter écharde *f*
split up se séparer
spoil gâter
sponge éponge *f*
spoon cuillère *f*
sport sport *m*
sports ground terrain *m* de sport
sporty sportif *m*, sportive *f*
spot *(place)* emplacement *m; (pimple)* bouton *m*; **on the spot** sur place
sprain: to sprain one's ankle se fouler la cheville
spring printemps *m*
square place *f*
stadium stade *m*
stain tache *f*
stained-glass windows vitraux *mpl*
stairs escalier *m*
stamp timbre *m* **95**
stand *(n)* stand *m*
start commencer

state état *m*
statement déclaration *f*
station gare *f*
stay *(n)* séjour *m*
stay *(v)* rester; **to stay in touch** rester en contact
steal voler **113**
step marche *f*
sticking plaster sparadrap *m*
still encore, toujours
still water eau *f* plate
sting *(n)* piqûre *f*
sting *(v)* piquer; **to get stung (by)** se faire piquer (par)
stock: out of stock épuisé(e)
stomach estomac *m; (belly)* ventre *m*
stone pierre *f*
stop *(n)* arrêt *m* **28**; *(v)* arrêter, s'arrêter
stopcock robinet *m* d'arrêt
storm orage *m*, tempête *f*
story histoire *f*
straight ahead, straight on tout droit
strange bizarre
street rue *f*
strong fort(e)
stuck bloqué(e), coincé(e)
student étudiant(e) *m,f* **15, 23**
studies études *fpl*
study étudier; **to study biology** faire des études de biologie
style style *m*
subtitled sous-titré(e)
suburb(s) banlieue *f*
suffer souffrir
suggest proposer
suit: does that suit you? ça vous va ?; **that suits you** ça vous va bien
suitcase valise *f* **25**
summer été *m*
sun soleil *m*; **in the sun** au soleil
sunbathe bronzer
sunburnt: to get sunburnt prendre un coup de soleil

sun cream crème f solaire
Sunday dimanche m
sunglasses lunettes fpl de soleil
sunhat chapeau m de soleil
sunrise lever m du soleil
sunset coucher m du soleil
sunstroke insolation f; **to get sunstroke** attraper une insolation
supermarket supermarché m **39**, **82**
supplement supplément m
sure sûr(e); (yes) bien sûr
surf surfer
surfboard planche f de surf
surfing surf m; **to go surfing** faire du surf
surgical spirit alcool m à 90°
surname nom m de famille
surprise (n) surprise f; (v) étonner
sweat transpirer
sweater pull m
sweet (n) bonbon m; (adj) sucré(e)
swim: (n) **to go for a swim** se baigner
swim (v) nager
swimming natation f
swimming pool piscine f
swimming trunks slip m de bain
swimsuit maillot m de bain
switchboard operator standardiste mf
switch off éteindre
switch on allumer
swollen enflé(e)
syrup sirop m

T

table table f **44**
tablespoon cuillère f à soupe
tablet comprimé m
take prendre; (to/from a place) emmener, emporter; **it takes 2 hours** ça prend 2 heures
takeaway à emporter
take off (plane) décoller
talk parler

tall grand(e)
tampon tampon m
tan bronzer
tanned bronzé(e)
tap robinet m
taste (n) goût m; (v) goûter
tax taxe f
tax-free hors taxes **31**
taxi taxi m **31**
taxi driver chauffeur m de taxi
T-bar tire-fesses m
team équipe f
teaspoon cuillère f à café
teenager adolescent(e) m,f
telephone (n) téléphone m; (v) téléphoner (à)
telephone directory annuaire m
television télévision f
tell raconter
tell off engueuler
temperature température f; **to have a temperature** avoir de la fièvre; **to take one's temperature** prendre sa température
temple temple m
temporary temporaire
tennis tennis m
tennis court court m de tennis
tennis shoes tennis fpl
tent tente f
tent peg sardine f
terminal terminal m
terrace terrasse f
terrible terrible
text message SMS m
thank remercier; **thank you** merci; **thank you very much** merci beaucoup
thanks merci; **thanks to** grâce à
that cela, ça; ce m, cette f; que; **that one** celui-là m, celle-là f
the le, la, les (see grammar)
theatre théâtre m
theft vol m

their leur, leurs *(see grammar)*
theirs le/la leur, les leurs *(see grammar)*
them les; eux; leur *(see grammar)*
theme park parc *m* d'attractions
then alors, ensuite
there y, là; **there is** il y a; **there are** il
  y a; **there is a castle** il y a un château;
  there are two museums il y a deux
  musées
therefore donc
thermometer thermomètre *m*
Thermos® flask thermos® *m*
these ces; **these ones** ceux-ci *m*,
  celles-ci *f*
they ils, elles; les *(see grammar)* **they
  say that …** on dit que …
thief voleur *m*, voleuse *f*
thigh cuisse *f*
thin maigre
thing chose *f*; **things** affaires *fpl*
think penser, croire, réfléchir
think about penser à
thirst soif *f*
thirsty: to be thirsty avoir soif
this cela, ça; ce *m*, cette *f*; **this one**
  celui-ci *m*, celle-ci *f*; **this evening** ce
  soir; **this is …** je te présente …
those ces; **those ones** ceux-là *m*,
  celles-là *f*
throat gorge *f*
throw jeter
throw out jeter, mettre à la poubelle
Thursday jeudi *m*
ticket *(for train, plane, show)* billet *m*
  23, **64**; *(for bus, underground)* ticket *m*
ticket office billetterie *f*
tidy ranger
tie cravate *f*
tight serré(e)
tights collant(s) *mpl*
time temps *m* **120**; fois *f*; **what time
  is it?** quelle heure est-il ?; **from time
  to time** de temps en temps; **to have
  (the) time to …** avoir le temps de

…; **on time** à l'heure; **three/four
  times** trois/quatre fois
time difference décalage *m* horaire
timetable horaires *mpl* **23**
tinfoil papier *m* alu
tip pourboire *m*
tired fatigué(e)
tobacco tabac *m*
tobacconist's bureau *m* de tabac
today aujourd'hui
together ensemble
toilet toilettes *fpl*, WC *mpl* **8**
toilet bag trousse *f* de toilette
toilet paper papier *m* toilette
toiletries affaires *fpl* de toilette
toll péage *m*
tomorrow demain; **tomorrow
  evening** demain soir
tongue langue *f*
tonight ce soir
too aussi, trop; **too bad** tant pis; **too
  many** trop de; **too much** trop de
tooth dent *f*
toothbrush brosse *f* à dents
toothpaste dentifrice *m*
top haut *m*; **at the top** en haut
torch lampe *f* de poche
touch toucher
tourist touriste *mf*
tourist office office *m* de tourisme
tourist trap attrape-touristes *m*
towards vers
towel serviette *f*; **bath/beach towel**
  serviette *f* de bain/de plage
town ville *f*
town centre centre-ville *m*
town hall mairie *f*, hôtel *m* de ville
toy jouet *m*
traditional traditionnel *m*, traditionnelle
  f, folklorique
traffic circulation *f*
traffic jam bouchon *m*, embouteillage
  m **29**
trailer bande-annonce *f*

train train *m* **27**; **the train to Avignon** le train en direction d'Avignon

train station gare *f*

tram tramway *m*

transfer *(of money)* virement *m*

translate traduire

travel voyager; **to travel alone** voyager seul

travel agency agence *f* de voyages

traveller's cheque Traveller's Cheque® *m*, chèque *m* de voyage

trip voyage *m*; excursion *f*; **have a good trip!** bon voyage !

trolley Caddie® *m*, chariot *m*

trouble: to have trouble doing something avoir du mal à faire quelque chose

trousers pantalon *m*

true vrai(e)

try essayer **85**; **to try to do something** essayer de faire quelque chose

try on essayer

tube métro *m*

tube station station *f* de métro

Tuesday mardi *m*

tupperware tupperware *m*

turn: *(n)* **it's your turn** c'est ton tour

turn *(v)* tourner

twice deux fois

type *(n)* type *m*; *(v)* taper

typical typique

tyre pneu *m*

umbrella parapluie *m*

uncle oncle *m*

uncomfortable pas à l'aise

under sous

underground métro *m*

underground line ligne *f* de métro

underground station station *f* de métro

underneath dessous

understand comprendre **10**

underwear sous-vêtements *mpl*

United Kingdom Royaume-Uni *m*

United States États-Unis *mpl*

until jusqu'à

upset *(distressed)* affecté(e); *(annoyed)* contrarié(e); *(offended)* vexé(e)

upstairs en haut, là-haut

urgent urgent(e)

us nous

use se servir de, utiliser; **to be used for** servir à; **I'm used to it** j'ai l'habitude; **I'm not used to eating so early** je n'ai pas l'habitude de manger aussi tôt

useful utile

useless inutile

usually d'habitude

U-turn demi-tour *m*

vaccinated (against) vacciné(e) (contre)

valid en cours de validité; **valid (for)** valable (pour)

valley vallée *f*

VAT TVA *f*

vegetarian végétarien *m*, végétarienne *f*

very très

view vue *f*

village village *m*

visa visa *m*

visit *(n)* visite *f*; *(v)* *(place)* visiter; *(person)* rendre visite à

volleyball volley(-ball) *m*

vomit vomir

W

waist taille *f*

wait attendre; **to wait for somebody/something** attendre quelqu'un/quelque chose

waiter serveur m

waitress serveuse f

wake up (se) réveiller

walk: (n) **to go for a walk** aller se promener, se balader

walk (v) marcher; (go for a walk) se promener

walking: to go walking faire de la marche

walking boots chaussures fpl de marche

Walkman® Walkman® m

wallet portefeuille m

want vouloir; **to want to do something** avoir envie de faire quelque chose

warm chaud(e); (welcome etc) chaleureux m, chaleureuse f

warn prévenir

wash: (n) **to have a wash** se laver

wash (v) laver; **to wash one's hair** se laver les cheveux

washbasin lavabo m

washing: to do the washing faire la lessive

washing machine machine f à laver

washing powder lessive f

washing-up liquid liquide m vaisselle

wasp guêpe f

waste gâcher; **to waste time** perdre du temps

watch (n) montre f

watch (v) regarder; **watch out!** attention!

water eau f **45**

water heater chauffe-eau m

waterproof imperméable m

waterproof jacket K-way® m

waterskiing ski m nautique

wave vague f

way (route) chemin m; (manner) façon f, manière f

way in entrée f

way out sortie f

we nous

weak faible

wear porter

weather temps m **21**; **the weather's bad** il fait mauvais

weather forecast prévisions fpl météo **21**

website site m Internet

Wednesday mercredi m

week semaine f

weekend week-end m

welcome bienvenu(e); **welcome!** bienvenue !; **you're welcome** il n'y a pas de quoi

well bien; **I'm very well** je vais bien; **well done** bien cuit; **well done!** bravo !

well-known connu(e)

west ouest m; **in the west** à l'ouest; **(to the) west of** à l'ouest de

wet mouillé(e)

wetsuit combinaison f de plongée

what qu'est-ce que, quoi; **what do you want?** que veux-tu ?; **what I liked most** ce que j'ai le plus aimé

wheel roue f

wheelchair fauteuil m roulant

when quand

where où; **where is/are …?** où est/sont … ?; **where are you from?** d'où viens-tu ?; **where are you going?** où vas-tu ?

which quel m, quelle f

while pendant que

whisky whisky m

white (adj) blanc m, blanche f; (n) blanc m

who qui; **who's calling?** qui est à l'appareil ?

whole entier m, entière f; **the whole cake** le gâteau en entier

whose dont

why pourquoi

wide large

wife femme f

wild sauvage
wind vent *m*
window fenêtre *f*, vitre *f*; **in the window** en vitrine **85**
windscreen pare-brise *m*
windsurfing planche *f* à voile
wine vin *m* **45**
winter hiver *m*
with avec
withdraw retirer
without sans
woman femme *f*
wonderful formidable
wood bois *m*
wool laine *f*
work *(n)* travail *m*
work *(v)* travailler; *(function)* marcher; **to work in** travailler dans
work of art œuvre *f* d'art
works travaux *mpl*
world monde *m*
worry *(n)* souci *m*; *(v)* s'inquiéter
worse pire; **to get worse** s'aggraver; **it's worse (than)** c'est pire (que)
worth: to be worth valoir; **it's worth it** ça vaut la peine; **it's worth …** ça vaut …
wound plaie *f*

wrist poignet *m*
write écrire **10**, **83**
wrong faux *m*, fausse *f*; **to be wrong** avoir tort

XYZ

X-rays rayons X *mpl*

year an *m*, année *f*
yellow *(adj)* jaune; *(n)* jaune *m*
yes oui
yesterday hier; **yesterday evening** hier soir
you tu, vous; te, vous; toi, vous *(see grammar)*
young jeune
your ton, ta, tes, votre, vos *(see grammar)*
yours le tien, la tienne, les tiens/tiennes, le/la vôtre, les vôtres *(see grammar)*
youth hostel auberge *f* de jeunesse

zero zéro *m*
zip fermeture *f* Éclair®
zoo zoo *m*
zoom (lens) zoom *m*

DICTIONARY

FRENCH-ENGLISH

A

à: aller à Paris/à la gare to go to Paris/to the station; **être à Paris** to be in Paris; **à 2 km** 2 km away; **à 3 heures** at 3 o'clock
abbaye abbey
abeille bee
abîmé damaged
abord: d'abord first (of all)
abordable affordable
accepter to accept
accès access
accident accident
accompagner to go with; to come with; to take
accord: d'accord OK; **je suis d'accord** I agree
accueil reception; information
accueillant welcoming
acheter to buy
adaptateur adaptor
addition bill
adolescent teenager
adorer to love
adresse address
adresse électronique e-mail address
adulte adult
aéroport airport
affaires business; things; **pour affaires** on business
affiche poster
Afrique Africa
âge age; **quel âge as-tu ?** how old are you?
agence de voyages travel agency

aggraver: s'aggraver to get worse
agréable nice
agresser to attack
aide help
aider to help
ailleurs somewhere else; **d'ailleurs** anyway
aimer to like; to love; **j'aimerais …** I'd like …
air air; **en plein air** outside; **avoir l'air …** to look …
aise: à l'aise comfortable; **pas à l'aise** uncomfortable
alcool alcohol
alcool à 90° surgical spirit
algues seaweed
Allemagne Germany
Allemand German
aller (n) outward journey; **un aller (simple)** a single (ticket)
aller (v) to go; **s'en aller** to go (away); **comment allez-vous ?** how are you?; **je vais bien** I'm very well; **ça va ?** how are you?; **ça va** I'm fine; **ça vous va ?** does that suit you?; **ça vous va bien** that suits you
allergique allergic
aller-retour return (ticket)
allô hello
allumer to light; to switch on
allumette match
alors so; then
ambassade embassy
ambiance atmosphere
ambulance ambulance
amende fine

amener to bring

américain American

ami(e) friend; **petit ami** boyfriend; **petite amie** girlfriend

amour love

amoureux: être amoureux (de) to be in love with (with); **tomber amoureux (de)** to fall in love (with)

ampoule (light) bulb; blister

amusant funny

amuser: s'amuser to enjoy oneself

an year; **j'ai 22 ans** I'm 22 (years old)

ancien old; former

anesthésie anaesthetic

angine sore throat

anglais English, British

Angleterre England

animal domestique pet

animé busy

année year; **bonne année !** Happy New Year!

anniversaire birthday; anniversary; **bon anniversaire !** happy birthday!

anniversaire de mariage wedding anniversary

annuaire phone book

annulé cancelled

annuler to cancel

antibiotique antibiotic

antiquité antique

août August

apéritif aperitif; **prendre l'apéritif** to have a drink before lunch/dinner

appareil: qui est à l'appareil ? who's calling?

appareil photo camera

appartement flat

appel call

appeler to call; **s'appeler** to be called; **je m'appelle ...** my name is ...

appendicite appendicitis

appétit: bon appétit ! enjoy your meal!

apporter to bring

apprendre to learn; to hear

après after

après-demain the day after tomorrow

après-midi afternoon

appuyer to press; **appuyer sur quelque chose** to press something

araignée spider

argent money; silver

arnaque rip-off

arrêt stop; **sans arrêt** continuously

arrêt de bus bus stop

arrêter to stop; **s'arrêter** to stop

arrivée arrival

arriver to arrive; to happen; **arriver à** to manage to; to reach

art art

artisanal traditionally made

article article; item

artisan craftsman

artiste artist

ascenseur lift

Asie Asia

aspirine aspirin

asseoir: s'asseoir to sit down

assez enough; quite; **assez de** enough

assiette plate

assurance insurance

assurance tous risques comprehensive insurance

asthme asthma

attendre to wait; **attendre quelqu'un/quelque chose** to wait for somebody/something

attention: faire attention to be careful; **attention !** watch out!, be careful!

attrape-touristes tourist trap

auberge de jeunesse youth hostel

aucun(e) *(adj)* no, not any; **aucune idée** no idea

aucun *(pron)* none

aujourd'hui today

aussi too, also; **moi aussi** me too; **aussi bien que** as well as

auteur author
autobus bus
autocar coach
automne autumn
autoroute motorway
autre other; **un(e) autre** another; **d'autres** others; **autre chose** something else
avance: à l'avance in advance; **en avance** early
avant before; **avant de faire** before doing
avant-hier the day before yesterday
avec with
avenue avenue
aveugle blind
avion plane; **par avion** airmail
avis opinion; **changer d'avis** to change one's mind
avoir to have
avril April

B

bagages luggage, baggage
bagages à main hand luggage
baigner: se baigner to go for a swim
bain bath; **prendre un bain** to have a bath
balader: se balader to go for a walk; to go for a drive
balcon balcony
balle ball
ballon ball
banlieue suburb(s)
banque bank
baptême christening
bas *(n)* bottom; **en bas** at the bottom; downstairs
bas *(adj)* low
basilique basilica
baskets trainers
basse low
bateau boat

bâtiment building
bâton stick
bâton de ski ski pole
batterie battery
bavarder to chat
beau beautiful; handsome
beaucoup (de) a lot (of), many; **beaucoup plus** much more, a lot more
bébé baby
belge Belgian
Belgique Belgium
belle beautiful
besoin: avoir besoin de to need
beurre butter
biberon (baby's) bottle
bibliothèque library
bicyclette bicycle
bien *(adv)* well; *(adj)* good; **j'aimerais bien …** I'd (really) like …
bien sûr of course
bientôt soon; **à bientôt !** see you soon!
bienvenu welcome; **bienvenue !** welcome!
bière beer
bijouterie jeweller's
bijoux jewellery
billet ticket; (bank)note
billetterie ticket office
bio organic
bise kiss; **faire la bise à quelqu'un** to kiss somebody on both cheeks
blanc white
blanche white
blessé injured
bleu blue; bruise; *(steak)* very rare
blond blond
bloqué stuck
blouson jacket
boire to drink
bois wood
boisson drink
boîte box

boîte aux lettres letterbox; postbox
boîte de conserve can
boîte de nuit (night)club
boîte de vitesses gearbox
bol bowl
bon good; right; **bon marché** cheap
bondé packed
bonjour hello; good morning; good afternoon
bonne good
bonsoir hello; good evening
bord: au bord de la mer at the seaside
bosse bump
bottes boots
bouche mouth
boucherie butcher's
bouchon cork; traffic jam
boucles d'oreilles earrings
bouée buoy
bougie candle; spark plug
boulangerie baker's
boule bowl; scoop
boules bowls
boules Quiès® earplugs
bout: un bout de … a bit of …; **au bout de deux heures** after two hours; **au bout de la rue** at the end of the street
bouteille bottle
bouteille de gaz gas cylinder
boutique shop
bouton button; spot
bracelet bracelet
branché trendy
brancher to plug in
bras arm
briquet lighter
bronchite bronchitis
bronzé tanned
bronzer to tan; to sunbathe
brosse brush; hairbrush
brosse à dents toothbrush
brouillard fog

bruit noise; **faire du bruit** to make a noise
brûler to burn; **se brûler** to burn oneself
brûlure burn
brun brown
bruyant noisy
bureau de poste post office
bureau de tabac tobacconist's
bus bus
but goal; aim

C

ça that; this; it
cabine d'essayage changing room
cabine téléphonique phone box
cadeau present
Caddie® trolley
cafard cockroach
café (black) coffee; café
café au lait white coffee
café crème white coffee, latte
café Internet Internet café
cahier notebook
caisse box; cashdesk, checkout
caleçon boxer shorts; swimming trunks
calme quiet
caméra camera
camion lorry
campagne country(side)
camping camping; campsite; **faire du camping** to go camping
camping-car camper
camping-gaz® camping stove
capitale capital
car coach
carafe jug
caravane caravan
cardiaque cardiac
carie: avoir une carie to have a cavity
carnet de tickets book of tickets
carte menu; map; card; **jouer aux cartes** to play cards

Carte Bleue® debit card
carte de crédit credit card
carte de téléphone phonecard
carte d'identité identity card
carte postale postcard
cas: au cas où just in case; **au cas où ...** in case ...; **en cas de ...** in case of ...
casque helmet
casquette cap
cassé broken
casse-croûte snack
casser to break; to split up; **se casser la jambe** to break one's leg
casserole (sauce)pan
catastrophe disaster
cathédrale cathedral
catholique (Roman) Catholic
cause: à cause de because of
caution deposit
ce this; that
ceinture belt
ceinture de sécurité seatbelt
cela that
célèbre famous
celle-ci this one
celle-là that one
celui-ci this one
celui-là that one
cendrier ashtray
centime d'euro euro cent
centimètre centimetre
centre centre
centre commercial shopping centre
centre-ville town centre
certain certain
ces these; those
c'est it's; **c'est très bon** it's very good; **c'est annulé** it's been cancelled
cette this; that
ceux-ci these ones
ceux-là those ones
chacun each one
chaîne chain; hi-fi; (TV) channel

chaise chair
chaleur heat
chaleureux warm
chambre room
chambre à air inner tube
chambres d'hôte bed and breakfast
chance luck; **bonne chance !** good luck!; **avoir de la chance** to be lucky
changement change
changer to change; **se changer** to get changed, to change
chapeau hat
chapeau de soleil sunhat
chapelle chapel
chaque each, every
charcuterie pork butcher's; cooked/cured meats
chariot trolley
chasse d'eau flush
château castle
chaud hot; **il fait chaud** it's hot; **boissons chaudes** hot drinks
chauffage heating
chauffe-eau water heater
chauffeur de taxi taxi driver
chaussettes socks
chaussures shoes
chaussures de marche walking boots
chaussures de ski ski boots
chef boss
chemin path; way
cheminée fireplace; chimney
chemise shirt
chemise de nuit nightdress
chèque cheque
chèque de voyage traveller's cheque
cher expensive; dear
chercher to look for; **aller chercher quelqu'un/quelque chose** to go and fetch somebody/something
cheval horse
cheveux hair
cheville ankle

chez: chez lui at/to his house; **je rentre chez moi** I'm going home
chinois Chinese
choc shock
choisir to choose
choix choice
choquant shocking
chose thing
ciel sky
cigare cigar
cigarette cigarette
cimetière cemetery
cinéma cinema
cintre coathanger
circulation traffic; circulation
cirque circus
ciseaux scissors
clair light; **bleu clair** light blue
classe class; **première/deuxième classe** first/second class
classique classic; classical
clé key
clignotant indicator
climat climate
climatisation air conditioning
cochon pig
code code
code confidentiel PIN (number)
code d'entrée door code
code postal postcode
cœur heart
coffre boot; chest
coiffeur hairdresser
coin corner; **un coin magnifique** a beautiful spot; **dans le coin** around here, in the area
coincé stuck
colère: en colère angry
colis parcel
collant(s) tights
colle glue
colline hill
colonie colony
colonie de vacances holiday camp

combien how many/much?; **combien ça coûte ?** how much is it?; **combien de temps … ?** how long …?; **depuis combien de temps … ?** for how long …?; **on est le combien ?** what's today's date?
combinaison de plongée wetsuit
commander to order
comme like, as
commencer to start, to begin
comment how; **comment ?** pardon?
commerces shops
commissariat (central) police station
communiquer to communicate
compagnie aérienne airline
compartiment compartment
complet whole; full; wholemeal
comprendre to understand
comprimé tablet
compris included; **tout compris** all inclusive
comptant: payer comptant to pay cash
compte account
compte bancaire bank account
compter to count
compteur électrique electricity meter
concert concert
conduire to drive; to take
confirmer to confirm
confortable comfortable
congélateur freezer
connaître to know
connu well-known
conseil: un conseil a piece of advice; **des conseils** advice; **demander conseil à quelqu'un** to ask somebody's advice
conseiller to advise
consigne left-luggage office
consommer to drink
consommation drink
constipé constipated
consulat consulate
contact contact; **rester en contact** to stay in touch

contacter to contact
contagieux contagious
contemporain contemporary
content pleased
continuer to continue, to go on;
  continuer à faire quelque chose to
  carry on doing something
continuation: bonne continuation !
  all the best!
contraceptif contraceptive
contraire opposite; **au contraire** on
  the contrary
contrat contract
contre against
coordonnées address and telephone
  number
copain friend; **petit copain** boyfriend
copine friend; **petite copine** girlfriend
corbeille basket
corps body
correspondance connection
côté side; **à côté de** beside
côte coast; rib; chop
coton cotton; cotton wool
coton-tige® cotton bud
cou neck
couche nappy
coucher: se coucher to go to bed; to
  lie down; **coucher avec** to sleep with
coucher du soleil sunset
couette quilt, duvet
couleur colour
coup: ça vaut le coup it's worth it;
  aller boire un coup to go for a drink
**coup de soleil: prendre un coup de
  soleil** to get sunburnt
coupe-ongles nail clippers
couper to cut; **se couper** to cut
  oneself; **coupé en tranches** sliced
courage courage; **bon courage !**
  good luck!
courant: être au courant (de) to
  know (about)
courrier mail, post

cours class, course
courses shopping; **faire des/les
  courses** to do some/the shopping
court short
cousin cousin
couteau knife
coûter to cost; **combien ça coûte ?**
  how much is it?
couverture blanket; cover
couvrir to cover
cravate tie
crayon pencil
crème cream
crème à raser shaving cream
crème hydratante moisturizer
crème solaire sun cream
crevé burst; exhausted
crise cardiaque heart attack
crise d'appendicite appendicitis
croire to believe; to think
croisière cruise
cru raw
cuillère spoon
cuillère à café teaspoon
cuillère à soupe tablespoon
cuire to cook; to bake
cuisine cooking; kitchen; **faire la
  cuisine** to do the cooking
cuisinier cook
cuisinière cooker; cook
cuisse thigh
cuit cooked; **bien cuit** well done; **trop
  cuit** overdone
culotte pants, knickers
culte (Protestant) church service
cybercafé Internet café

D

dangereux dangerous
dans in; **dans une heure** in an hour;
  dans la soirée in the evening
danse dance
danser to dance

date date
date de naissance date of birth
date d'expiration expiry date
date limite deadline
dater (de) to date (from)
de of; from; **le vélo de David** David's bike; **de ... à ...** from ... to ...; **du pain** (some) bread; **des œufs** (some) eggs
dé dice
début beginning, start; **au début** at the beginning
débutant beginner
décalage horaire time difference; jetlag
décapsuleur bottle opener
décembre December
décevant disappointing
décider to decide
déclaration statement
déclarer to declare
décoller to take off
déçu disappointed
dedans inside
défaut flaw
dégonflé flat
degré degree
dehors outside
déjà already; yet
déjeuner (n) lunch; (v) to have lunch
demain tomorrow; **à demain !** see you tomorrow!; **demain soir** tomorrow evening
demander to ask
démanger: ça me démange it's itchy
demi half; **un demi-litre/-kilo** half a litre/kilo; **une demi-heure** half an hour; **une heure et demie** an hour and a half; **un demi** (beer) a half-pint
demi-tour U-turn
demi-pension half-board
dent tooth
dentifrice toothpaste
dentiste dentist

déodorant deodorant
dépannage: service de dépannage breakdown service
départ departure
dépêcher: se dépêcher to hurry (up)
dépendre: ça dépend (de) it depends (on)
dépenser to spend
dépliant leaflet
déposer: déposer quelqu'un to drop somebody off
depuis since; **depuis que** since; **depuis quand êtes-vous ici ?** how long have you been here?
déranger to disturb
dernier last; **au dernier moment** at the last minute; **l'année dernière** last year
derrière behind
des see de
dès from; **dès que** as soon as
désagréable unpleasant
descendre to go down; to get off
désert desert
désinfecter to disinfect
désolé sorry
dessert dessert
dessous underneath; **en dessous (de)** below
dessus above; **au-dessus (de)** above
destinataire addressee
détendre: se détendre to relax
détester to hate
devant in front of
développer: faire développer une pellicule to get a film developed
devenir to become
devise currency
devoir to have to; to owe; **je dois y aller** I have to go, I must go; **il doit être 5 heures** it must be 5 o'clock; **vous devriez ...** you should ...
diabète diabetes
diapositive slide

diarrhée: avoir la diarrhée to have diarrhoea
diesel diesel
différent (de) different (from)
difficile (à) difficult (to)
dimanche Sunday
diminuer to reduce
dîner *(n)* dinner; *(v)* to have dinner
dire to say; **vouloir dire** to mean; **comment dit-on … ?** how do you say …?; **ça te dit de … ?** do you feel like …?
direct direct
directement directly
direction direction; management; **le train en direction de Toulouse** the train to Toulouse
discothèque disco
disque record
distributeur (automatique de billets) cashpoint
docteur doctor
document document
doigt finger
dommage: c'est dommage it's a pity
donc so, therefore
donner to give
dont whose; **l'hôtel dont il me parlait** the hotel he told me about
dormir to sleep; **dormir à la belle étoile** to sleep out in the open
dos back
douane customs
doublé dubbed
doucement gently; softly; slowly
douche shower; **prendre une douche** to take a shower
drap sheet
drogue drug
droit *(n)* right; *(adj)* right; **le côté droit** the right-hand side; **avoir le droit de …** to have the right to …; **tout droit** straight on, straight ahead
droite right; **à droite (de)** to the right (of)

drôle funny
du see de
dur hard
durer to last

eau water
échanger to exchange
écharde splinter
écharpe scarf
écouter to listen; **écouter quelqu'un/quelque chose** to listen to someone/something
écrire to write
effort effort; **faire un effort** to make an effort
égal equal; **ça m'est égal** I don't mind
église church
électrique electric
elle she; it
elles they; them
embarquement boarding
embarquer to board
embouteillage traffic jam
embrayage clutch
émission programme
emmener to take
emplacement spot, place
emporter to take; **à emporter** takeaway
emprunter to borrow
en in; **en France/2005/anglais** in France/2005/English; **je vais en France** I'm going to France; **en voiture** by car
enceinte pregnant
enchanté! pleased to meet you!
encore still; more; again; **pas encore** not yet; **encore plus** even more
endormir: s'endormir to fall asleep
enfant child
enfin finally
enflé swollen

engueuler to shout at; **s'engueuler** to have a row

enlever to remove

ennuyer: s'enuyer to be bored

enregistrement check-in

enregistrer to check in

enrhumé: être enrhumé to have a cold

ensemble together

ensuite then, next

entendre to hear

entier whole; **le gâteau en entier** the whole cake

entracte interval, intermission

entre between; **entre midi et deux** between midday and two

entrée entrance, way in; starter; admission

entrer to go in; to come in

enveloppe envelope

envie: avoir envie de to want to

environ about, around; **dans les environs** in the area

envoyer to send

épaule shoulder

épicé spicy, hot

épicerie grocer's

éponge sponge

épuisé exhausted; out of stock

équipe team

erreur mistake

escalade climbing

escalier stairs

Espagne Spain

espagnol Spanish

espérer to hope; **j'espère que …** I hope …

essayer to try; to try on; **essayer de faire quelque chose** to try to do something

essence petrol

est east; **à l'est** in the east; **à l'est de** (to the) east of

estomac stomach

et and

étage floor

état state

États-Unis United States

été summer

éteindre to put out; to switch off

éternuer to sneeze

étonner to surprise

étranger *(adj)* foreign; *(n)* foreigner; **à l'étranger** abroad

être to be; **je suis Écossais** I'm Scottish; **est-ce que tu es content ?** are you happy?; **c'est beau** it's beautiful

études studies; **faire des études de biologie** to study biology

étudiant student

euro euro

eurochèque Eurocheque

Europe Europe

européen European

eux them

évanouir: s'évanouir to faint

évident obvious

excédent excess; **j'avais un excédent de bagages de cinq kilos** my luggage was five kilos overweight

exceptionnel exceptional; **ça n'a rien d'exceptionnel** it's nothing special

excursion trip

excuse excuse

excuser: s'excuser to apologize; **excusez-moi** I'm sorry; excuse me

exemple example; **par exemple** for example

expéditeur sender

expliquer to explain

exposition exhibition

exprès on purpose

exprimer to express; **s'exprimer** to express oneself

fac university, uni
face: en face (de) opposite
fâché angry
facile (à) easy (to)
façon way; **de toute façon** anyway
facteur postman
facture bill
faible weak
faim hunger; **avoir faim** to be hungry
faire to do, to make; **ça ne fait rien** it doesn't matter
fait fact; **en fait** in fact; **au fait, …** by the way …; **fait main** handmade
falaise cliff
falloir: il faut faire attention you/we/etc must be careful; **il faut se dépêcher** we must hurry; **il me faut un stylo** I need a pen; **il faut que j'y aille** I must go; **il faut que vous le voyiez** you must see it
famille family
fatigant tiring
fatigué tired
faute mistake
fauteuil roulant wheelchair
faux wrong; false
félicitations ! congratulations!
femme woman; wife
fenêtre window
fer à repasser iron
férié: jour férié public holiday; **lundi est férié** Monday is a public holiday
fermé closed, shut
fermer to close, to shut; **fermer à clé** to lock
fermeture closing; **heure de fermeture** closing time
fermeture Éclair® zip
fesses bottom
festival festival
fête party; **faire la fête** to celebrate; to have a good time

fête foraine funfair
fête nationale national holiday
feu fire; **tu as du feu ?** do you have a light?; **au feu !** fire!
feu rouge red light
feux d'artifice fireworks
février February
fiancé fiancé; **être fiancé** to be engaged
fiancée fiancée
fier (de) proud (of)
fièvre fever; **avoir de la fièvre** to have a temperature
fille girl; daughter
film film
fils son
fin *(n)* end; **à la fin de** at the end of
fin *(adj)* thin; fine
finalement finally
finir to finish
fleuve river
flic cop
foie liver
foire fair
fois time; **combien de fois … ?** how many times …?; **une/deux fois** once/twice
folklorique traditional
foncé dark; **bleu foncé** dark blue
fond bottom; **au fond de** at the bottom of; at the back of
forêt forest
forfait pass
formulaire form
fort strong; loud
foulard scarf
fouler: se fouler la cheville to sprain one's ankle
four oven
fourchette fork
fourmi ant
fourrière (car) pound
fragile fragile
frais cool; cold; chilly

français French
France France
frein brake
frein à main handbrake
freiner to brake
frère brother
Frigidaire® fridge
frigo fridge
froid cold; **il fait froid** it's cold; **avoir froid** to be cold; **prendre froid** to catch cold
front forehead
fruit piece of fruit; **fruits** fruit
frontière border
fuite leak
fumer to smoke
fumeur smoker; **fumeurs** smoking; **non-fumeurs** non-smoking
fusible fuse

G

gâcher to waste
gagner to earn; to save
galerie gallery
gant glove
gant de toilette facecloth
garage garage
garantie guarantee
garçon boy; waiter
garder to keep
gare (train) station
gare routière coach station
garer: se garer to park
gâter to spoil
gauche left; **à gauche (de)** to the left (of)
gaz gas
gazeux fizzy
gel frost; gel
gel douche shower gel
gendarme policeman
gendarmerie police station
généraliste GP

genou knee
genre: quel genre de … ? what kind of …?
gens people; **les gens** people
gentil nice
glace ice; ice cream; mirror
glaçon ice cube; **avec ou sans glaçons ?** with or without ice?
golf golf; golf course
gorge throat
gothique Gothic
gourde flask
goût taste
goûter (n) (afternoon) snack
goûter to taste; to have an afternoon snack
gouttes drops
grâce à thanks to
grammes grams
grand big; tall
Grande-Bretagne (Great) Britain
grandir to grow; **j'ai grandi en France** I grew up in France
grand-mère grandmother
grand-père grandfather
grands-parents grandparents
gras fat
grasse fat
gratte-ciel skyscraper
gratuit free
grave serious; **ce n'est pas grave** it doesn't matter
grec Greek
Grèce Greece
grippe flu
grippe intestinale gastric flu
gris grey
gros big
groupe group; **groupe de musique** band
guêpe wasp
guérir to get better
gueule de bois hangover
guide guidebook; guide

guide des spectacles listings magazine
gymnase gym
gynécologue gynaecologist

H

habiller: s'habiller to get dressed
habiter to live
habitude habit; **d'habitude** usually;
 j'ai l'habitude I'm used to it
hanche hip
handicapé disabled
haut *(n)* top; **en haut** at the top;
 upstairs
haut *(adj)* high
héberger to put up
hémorroïdes piles
herbe grass
hésiter to hesitate
heure hour; **à quelle heure … ?** what
 time …?; **à cinq heures** at five o'clock;
 à l'heure on time; **heure locale** local
 time; **à tout à l'heure** see you later
heureux happy
hier yesterday; **hier soir** yesterday
 evening, last night
histoire history; story
hiver winter
hollandais Dutch
Hollande Holland, the Netherlands
homéopathie homoeopathy
homme man
homosexuel homosexual
honnête honest
honte shame; **avoir honte** to be
 ashamed
hôpital hospital
horaires timetable
hors service out of order
hôtel hotel
hôtel de ville town hall
huile oil
**humeur: être de bonne/mauvaise
 humeur** to be in a good/bad mood

humide damp
humour humour
hypertension high blood pressure
hypotension low blood pressure

I

ici here; **d'ici un quart d'heure** in a
 quarter of an hour
il he; it
il y a: il y a un château there is a
 castle; **il y a deux musées** there are
 two museums; **il y a deux ans** two
 years ago
île island
ils they
immeuble building; block of flats
impatient impatient; **être impatient
 de …** to be looking forward to …
imperméable *(adj)* waterproof
imperméable *(n)* raincoat
important important
impossible impossible
imprimer to print
incendie fire
indépendant independent
indicatif dialling code
infection infection
infirmière nurse
informations information; news
inquiéter: s'inquiéter to worry
inscrire: s'inscrire to sign up
insecte insect
insecticide insecticide
insolation sunstroke
insomnie insomnia
instant: un instant, s'il vous plaît
 one moment, please
intention: avoir l'intention de to
 intend to
interdit forbidden
intérieur: à l'intérieur inside
intoxication alimentaire food
 poisoning

inutile useless; **inutile de …** no need to …
invité *(n)* guest
inviter to invite
Italie Italy
italien Italian

J

jamais never; **ne … jamais** never; **si jamais** if ever
jambe leg
janvier January
Japon Japan
japonais Japanese
jardin garden
jaune yellow
je I
jean jeans
jetable disposable
jeter to throw; to throw out
jeudi Thursday
jeune *(adj)* young
jeune *(n)* young person
jogging jogging; tracksuit
joli pretty
jouer to play; **jouer à** to play; **ça joue à …** it's on at …
jouet toy
jour day; **de nos jours** nowadays
journal newspaper
journée day
juillet July
juin June
jumelles binoculars
jupe skirt
jusqu'à until
juste fair; **juste avant/un peu** just before/a little

K

kilomètre kilometre
kiosque à journaux newsstand

K-way® waterproof jacket

L

la the; her; it
là there
là-bas over there
lac lake
là-haut up there; upstairs
laine wool
laisser to let; to leave; **laissez-moi tranquille** leave me alone; **laisser tomber** to drop
lait après-soleil after-sun
lait hydratant moisturizer
lame de rasoir razor blade
lampe lamp
lampe de poche torch
langue tongue; language
large wide
lavabo washbasin
lave-vaisselle dishwasher
laver to wash; **se laver** to have a wash; **se laver les dents** to clean one's teeth; **se laver les cheveux** to wash one's hair
laverie launderette
le the; him; it
léger light
lentement slowly
lentilles lentils; **lentilles (de contact)** contact lenses
les the; them
lessive washing powder
lettre letter
leur *(adj)* their; *(pron)* them; **leurs** their; **le/la leur, les leurs** theirs
lever: se lever to get up
levée collection
lever du soleil sunrise
lèvre lip
librairie bookshop
libre available; free
lieu place; **au lieu de** instead of

ligne line; **ligne de métro** underground line; **ligne de bus** bus route

linge sale (dirty) washing

liquide cash; **payer en liquide** to pay cash

liquide vaisselle washing-up liquid

lire to read

lit bed

litre litre

livre book

livre (sterling) pound

location rental, hire

logement accommodation

loin far; **loin de** far from

longtemps a long time

lorsque when

louer to rent, to hire

lourd heavy; close

loyer rent

lui him; her; it

lumière light

lundi Monday

lune moon

lune de miel honeymoon

lunettes glasses

lunettes de soleil sunglasses

luxe luxury; **... de luxe** luxury ...

M

ma my

machine à laver washing machine

Madame Mrs; Madam

Mademoiselle Miss

magasin shop; **grand magasin** department store

mai May

maigre thin

maillot de bain swimsuit; swimming trunks

main hand

maintenant now

mairie town hall

mais but

maison house; **à la maison** at home

mal (adj) bad; (adv) badly; **ça fait mal** it hurts; **avoir mal au cœur** to feel sick; **avoir mal à la tête/à la gorge/au ventre** to have a headache/a sore throat/a sore stomach; **avoir le mal de mer** to be seasick; **avoir du mal à faire quelque chose** to have trouble doing something; **c'est pas mal** it's not bad; **pas mal de** quite a lot of

malade ill

maladie illness

malentendu misunderstanding

maman mum, mummy

manche sleeve

Manche: la Manche the (English) Channel

mandat international international money order

manger to eat

manière way; **de toute manière** in any case

manquer to miss; **il manque deux ...** there are two ... missing; **il me manque deux ...** I'm two ... short; **tu me manques** I miss you

manteau coat

maquillage make-up

maquiller: se maquiller to put on one's make-up

marchand shopkeeper

marchand de journaux newsagent

marchandises goods

marche step; **faire de la marche** to go walking; **marche avant/arrière** forward/reverse gear

marché market

marcher to walk; to work

mardi Tuesday

marée basse/haute low/high tide

mari husband

mariage wedding; marriage

marié married

marre: en avoir marre (de) to be fed up (with)

marron brown; chestnut

mars March

match match

matelas mattress

matelas pneumatique airbed

matériel equipment

matin morning

mauvais bad; **il fait mauvais** the weather's bad

me me

mec guy

méchant bad

médecin doctor

médicament medicine

meilleur better; **le meilleur** the best; the better; **meilleur que …** better than …

mélanger to mix

membre member

même *(adj)* same; *(adv)* even; **même si** even if; **moi-même** myself; **lui-même** himself

ménage housework; **faire le ménage** to do the housework

mentir to lie

menton chin

menu set menu

mer sea; **la mer Méditerranée/du Nord** the Mediterranean/North Sea

merci thank you, thanks; **merci beaucoup** thank you very much; **non merci** no, thank you

mercredi Wednesday

mère mother

mes my

message message

messe mass

métier occupation

mètre metre

métro underground

mettre to put

micro-ondes microwave

midi midday, noon

mien: le mien/la mienne mine; **les miens/miennes** mine

mieux better; **mieux que …** better than …

mignon cute, pretty

milieu middle; **au milieu (de)** in the middle (of)

ministre minister

minuit midnight

minute minute

Mobylette® moped

moderne modern

moi me

moins less; **au moins** at least; **moins que** less than; **dix heures moins le quart** a quarter to ten

mois month

moitié half

moment moment; **un moment !** just a moment!; **en ce moment** at the moment; **pour le moment** for the moment; **à ce moment-là** then

mon my

monastère monastery

monde world; **tout le monde** everybody; **il y a du monde** there are lots of people

monnaie money; currency; change

Monsieur Mr; Sir

montagne mountain

montre watch

montrer to show

monument monument

morceau piece; **un morceau de** a piece of

morsure bite

mort *(adj)* dead; *(n)* dead

mosquée mosque

mot word; note

moteur engine

moto motorcycle, motorbike

mouche fly

mouchoir handkerchief

mouillé wet
moulin mill
mourir to die
mousse à raser shaving foam
moustique mosquito
moyen (n) way; (adj) average
mur wall
mûr ripe
muscle muscle
musée museum
musique music

N

nager to swim; **est-ce que tu sais nager?** can you swim?
naître: je suis né le/en ... I was born on the/in ...
natation swimming
nature nature
nausée: avoir la nausée to feel sick
navette shuttle
ne see **pas**, **plus**, **jamais**, **rien**
né see **naître**
nécessaire necessary
négatif negative
neige snow
neiger to snow
nerveux nervous
nettoyer to clean
neuf nine; new
neuve new
neveu nephew
nez nose
ni ... ni ... neither ... nor ...
nièce niece
nocturne (n) late-night opening
Noël Christmas; **joyeux Noël !** Merry Christmas!
noir black; **noir et blanc** black and white
nom name; surname
nombre number
nom de famille surname

nom de jeune fille maiden name
non no; **je ne fume pas — moi non plus** I don't smoke — neither do I
nord north; **au nord** in the north; **au nord de** (to the) north of
normal normal
nos our
note bill
noter to write down
notre our
nôtre: le/la nôtre ours; **les nôtres** ours
nourriture food
nous we; us
nouveau new; **de/à nouveau** again; **nouvel an** New Year
nouvelle (adj) new
nouvelle: (n) **bonne/mauvaise nouvelle** good/bad news; **les nouvelles** the news
novembre November
noyer: se noyer to drown
nu naked
nuage cloud
nuit night; **bonne nuit** goodnight
nul useless; **nulle part** nowhere
numéro number
numéro de téléphone phone number
numéro d'immatriculation registration number

O

objectif lens
occasion opportunity; **d'occasion** second-hand
occupé busy; engaged
occuper: s'occuper de to look after
océan ocean; **l'océan Atlantique** the Atlantic Ocean
octobre October
odeur smell
œil eye
œuf egg

œuvre d'art work of art
office de tourisme tourist office
offrir to offer; to give
oiseau bird
ombre shade; **à l'ombre** in the shade
on one; we; **on dit que ...** they say that ...
oncle uncle
ongle nail
opérer to operate; **se faire opérer** to have an operation
opticien optician
orage storm
orange orange
orchestre orchestra
ordinateur computer
ordinateur portable laptop
ordures rubbish
oreille ear
oreiller pillow
organiser to organize
origine origin; **être d'origine ...** to be of ... origin
ou or
où where; **où est/sont ... ?** where is/are?; **où vas-tu ?** where are you going?; **d'où viens-tu ?** where are you from?
oublier to forget
ouest west; **à l'ouest** in the west; **à l'ouest de** (to the) west of
oui yes
ouvert open
ouvre-boîtes can opener
ouvre-bouteilles bottle opener
ouvrir to open

P

page page
palais palace
pâle pale
panier basket
panne breakdown; **tomber en panne**
to break down; **être en panne d'essence** to have run out of petrol
panneau sign; road sign
pansement dressing, Elastoplast®
pantalon trousers
papa dad, daddy
papier paper
papier à cigarette cigarette paper
papier alu tinfoil
papier cadeau gift wrap
papiers d'identité identity papers
papier toilette toilet paper
Pâques Easter; **joyeuses Pâques !**
Happy Easter!
paquet packet; parcel
paraître: il paraît que ... it seems that ...
par by; **une fois par jour/heure** once a day/an hour
parapluie umbrella
parasol beach umbrella
parc park
parc d'attractions theme park
parce que because
pardon sorry; excuse me
pare-brise windscreen
pare-chocs bumper
pareil same
parents parents
parfum perfume; flavour
parking car park
parler to speak
parmi among
partager to share
partie part; **faire partie de** to be a part of
partir to leave; **à partir de ...** from ...
partout everywhere
pas: ne ... pas not; **pas du tout** not at all
passage: être de passage to be passing through
passager passenger
passé (n) past

passeport passport
passer to spend; **je suis passé vers 6 heures** I came by around 6 o'clock; **passer prendre quelqu'un** to go and pick somebody up; **passer un coup de téléphone** to make a phone call; **se passer de …** to go without …
patient patient
pâtisserie pastry; cake shop
patron boss
pauvre poor
payant: l'entrée est payante there's a charge for admission
payer to pay
pays country
paysage landscape; scenery
Pays-Bas Netherlands
PCV reverse charge call
péage toll
peau skin
pêcher to fish
peigne comb
peine: à peine hardly; **ça vaut la peine** it's worth it
peinture painting
peler to peel
pellicule film
pendant during; **pendant une heure** for an hour; **pendant que** while
pension complète full board
penser to think; **penser à** to think about
perdre to lose; **se perdre** to get lost; **être perdu** to be lost; **perdre du temps** to waste time
père father
périmé out of date
permettre to allow
permis de conduire driving licence
personne (n) person; (pron) nobody
petit small, little; **petit à petit** little by little
petit déjeuner (n) breakfast
peu not much; not very; few; **peu de** few, not many; little, not much; **un peu** a little; **un peu de vin** a little wine; **à peu près** almost; around
peuple people
peur fear; **avoir peur (de)** to be scared (of)
peut-être maybe, perhaps
phare lighthouse; headlight
pharmacie chemist's
pharmacie de garde duty chemist's
photo photo; **prendre quelqu'un en photo** to take somebody's photo; **prendre une/des photo(s)** to take a photo/photos
pièce coin; room
pièce de rechange spare part
pièce de théâtre play
pied foot; **aller à pied** to walk, to go on foot
pierre stone
piéton pedestrian; **rue piétonne** pedestrian street
pile battery; **trois heures pile** three o'clock on the dot
pilule pill; **prendre la pilule** to be on the pill
pilule du lendemain morning-after pill
pipe pipe
pipi pee; **faire pipi** to have a pee
pique-nique picnic
pique-niquer to have a picnic
piquer to sting; **se faire piquer (par)** to get stung (by)
piqûre injection; sting
pire worse; **c'est pire (que)** it's worse (than)
piscine swimming pool
piste cyclable cycle path
place seat; square; **il n'y a plus de place** there's no more room; there are no seats/tickets left; **sur place** on the spot
place de parking parking space
plage beach

plaie wound
plaindre: se plaindre to complain
plaire to please; **s'il te/vous plaît** please; **ça me plaît** I like it
plan map
planche à voile windsurfing
planche de surf surfboard
plante plant
plaque électrique hotplate
plat *(adj)* flat
plat *(n)* dish
plat du jour today's special
plat principal main course
plâtre: avoir la jambe dans le plâtre to have one's leg in plaster
plein full; **plein de** full of; **faire le plein (d'essence)** to fill up (with petrol)
pleuvoir: il pleut it's raining
plombage filling
plombier plumber
plongée (sous-marine) (scuba) diving; **faire de la plongée** to go diving
pluie rain
plupart: la plupart most; **la plupart des gens** most people
plus more; **il n'y a plus de ...** there's/there are no more ...; **il ne me reste plus que deux jours** I have only two days left; **ce que j'ai le plus aimé** what I liked most
plusieurs several
plutôt rather
pneu tyre
poêle frying pan
poignet wrist
poil hair
point point; **être sur le point de ...** to be about to ...; **à point** medium
pointure size
poisson fish
poissonnerie fishmonger's
poitrine chest
police police
policier policeman

pommade ointment
pompe à vélo bicycle pump
pompiers fire brigade
pont bridge
port port; harbour; **port de plaisance** marina
portable mobile (phone)
porte door; gate
portefeuille wallet
porte-monnaie purse
porter to carry; to wear
portrait portrait
portugais Portuguese
Portugal Portugal
poser to put; **poser une question** to ask a question
possible possible; **le plus tôt possible** as soon as possible
poste mail, post; post office
pot pot; jar
potable: eau potable drinking water; **eau non potable** non-drinking water
pot d'échappement exhaust (pipe)
poubelle (dust)bin; **mettre à la poubelle** to throw out
poudre powder
poumon lung
pour for; **pour que** so that; **pour cent** percent; **être pour quelque chose** to be in favour of something
pourboire tip
pourquoi why
pousser to push
poussette pushchair
pouvoir to be able to; **je ne peux pas** I can't; **on peut y aller demain** we can go tomorrow
pratique practical
précédent previous
préféré favourite
préférer to prefer
premier first
prendre to take; **ça prend deux heures** it takes two hours

prénom first name
préparer to prepare
près near; **(tout) près de** (right) beside
présenter to introduce; **je te présente …** this is …
préservatif condom
presque almost
pressé: être pressé to be in a hurry
pressing dry cleaner's
pression (draught) beer; pressure
prêt ready; **être prêt à** to be ready to
prêter to lend
prévenir to warn
prévisions météo weather forecast
prévoir to plan; to forecast
prier: je t'en/vous en prie you're welcome
principal main
printemps spring
prise socket; plug
privé private
prix price; prize
probablement probably
problème problem
prochain next; **à la prochaine !** see you (soon)!
proche near; **le plus proche** the nearest
produit product
profession profession
profiter de to make the most of
profond deep
promener: se promener to walk; **aller se promener** to go for a walk
promettre to promise
proposer to suggest
propre clean; own
propriétaire owner
protéger to protect; **se protéger** to protect oneself
prudent careful
public (adj) public; (n) public
puisque since

pull sweater, jumper
pyjama (pair of) pyjamas

quai platform; quay
qualité quality; **de bonne qualité** of good quality
quand when; **quand même** all the same
quart quarter; **un quart d'heure** a quarter of an hour
quartier area
que that; **ne … que** only; **que veux-tu ?** what do you want?; **qu'est-ce que … ?** what …?; **plus petit que** smaller than; **je pense que …** I think (that) …
quel what, which
quelque chose something
quelque part somewhere
quelquefois sometimes
quelques some
quelques-uns some
quelqu'un someone, somebody
question question; **poser une question** to ask a question
queue tail; queue; **faire la queue** to queue (up)
qui who
quitter to leave; **ne quittez pas** hold on
quoi what; **il n'y a pas de quoi** you're welcome
quoique although

rabais : faire un rabais à quelqu'un to give somebody a discount
raccourci short cut
raconter to tell
radiateur radiator
radio radio; X-ray

rage de dents severe toothache
raisonnable reasonable
râler to moan
randonnée hiking, hill-walking; **faire de la randonnée** to go hiking/hill-walking
ranger to tidy
rapide quick
rappeler to call back; **se rappeler** to remember; **ça me rappelle …** that reminds me of …
raquette racket
rare rare
rarement rarely
raser: se raser to shave
rasoir razor
rasoir électrique electric shaver
rater to miss
ravi delighted; **ravi de faire votre connaissance** pleased to meet you
rayon department
réception reception; signal; **à la réception** at reception
recette recipe
recevoir to receive, to get
rechange: … de rechange spare …
recharger to charge
recommandé: en recommandé registered
recommander to recommend
reconnaissant grateful
reconnaître to recognize
reçu receipt
réduction reduction
réfléchir to think
réfrigérateur fridge
refuge de montagne mountain hut
refuser to refuse
regarder to look at, to watch
régime diet; **être au régime** to be on a diet
région area; **dans la région** in the area
règles periods; **avoir ses règles** to be having one's period

rein kidney
rejoindre to meet
remarquer to notice
rembourser to refund; **se faire rembourser** to get a refund
remercier to thank
remontée mécanique ski lift
remplir to fill; to fill in/out
rencontrer to meet; **se rencontrer** to meet (each other)
rendez-vous appointment; date; **prendre un rendez-vous** to make an appointment; **se donner rendez-vous** to arrange to meet; **avoir rendez-vous (avec)** to meet; to have an appointment (with)
rendre to give back
renseignement information; **les renseignements** directory enquiries
rentrer to go home
renverser to knock over; **se faire renverser** to get knocked down
réparer to repair; **faire réparer** to get repaired
repas meal
repasser to iron
repère landmark; **point de repère** landmark
répéter to repeat
répondeur answering machine
répondre to answer
réponse answer
reposer: se reposer to rest
réservé reserved
réserver to book
ressembler à to look like
reste rest; **le reste** the rest
rester to stay; **est-ce qu'il reste des places ?** are there any tickets left?
retard delay; **en retard** late
retardé delayed
retirer to withdraw
retour return; **être de retour** to be back

retrait des bagages baggage reclaim
retrouver: se retrouver to meet
réunion meeting
réveil alarm clock
réveiller to wake up; **se réveiller** to wake up
revenir to come back
rêver to dream
revoir: au revoir goodbye
revoir: se revoir to see each other again
revue magazine
rez-de-chaussée ground floor
rhumatismes rheumatism
rhume cold
rhume des foins hay fever
riche rich
rien: ne rien nothing
rigoler to laugh; to joke
rire to laugh
risque risk
risquer: il risque de pleuvoir it might rain
rivière river
robe dress
rocher rock
rollers rollerblades
roman *(n)* novel
roman *(adj)* Romanesque
rond-point roundabout
robinet tap
robinet d'arrêt stopcock
rose pink; rose
roue wheel; **roue avant** front wheel
roue de secours spare wheel
rouge red
route road
rouvrir to reopen
Royaume-Uni United Kingdom
rue street
ruines ruins; **en ruines** in ruins

sa his; her
sable sand
sac bag
sac à dos backpack, rucksack
sac à main handbag
sac de couchage sleeping bag
sac plastique plastic bag
sac poubelle bin bag
saignant rare
saigner to bleed
saison season
sale dirty
salé salted; salty; savoury
salir to (get) dirty; **se salir** to get dirty
salle room
salle de cinéma auditorium
salle de concert concert hall
salle de bains bathroom
salon living room
salut! hi!; bye!
samedi Saturday
sandales sandals
sang blood
sans without
santé health; **être en bonne santé** to be in good health; **santé !** cheers!
sauf except
sauvage wild
sauvegarder to save
savoir to know; **sais-tu nager ?** can you swim?
savon soap
Scotch® Sellotape®
sec dry
sèche dry
sèche-cheveux hairdrier
sécher to dry; **faire sécher** to dry
seconde second
secours help; **au secours !** help!; **appeler au secours** to call for help
secrétaire secretary

sécurité security, safety; **en sécurité** secure, safe

sein breast

séjour stay

sel salt

semaine week; **en semaine** during the week; **toute la semaine** all week

sens direction; sense, meaning

sensible sensitive

sentier path

sentiment feeling

sentir to feel; to smell; **sentir bon/mauvais** to smell good/bad; **se sentir** to feel; **se sentir bien/mal** to feel good/bad

séparer to separate; **se séparer** to split up

septembre September

sérieux serious

serré tight

serrure lock

serveur barman; waiter

serveuse barmaid; waitress

service tip; favour; **rendre service à quelqu'un** to do somebody a favour

serviette towel; napkin

serviette de bain bath towel

serviette en papier paper napkin

serviette hygiénique sanitary towel

servir à to be used for; **se servir de** to use

ses his; her

seul only; alone; **un seul** just one; **voyager seul** to travel alone

seulement only

sexe sex

shampooing shampoo

shopping shopping; **aller faire du shopping** to go shopping

short (pair of) shorts

si so; if; yes

siècle century; **au XIXᵉ siècle** in the 19th century

sien: le sien/la sienne his; hers; **les**

siens/siennes his; hers

sieste nap; **faire la sieste** to have a nap

signer to sign

signifier to mean

silent silencieux

simple simple

sinon otherwise

sirop syrup

site Internet website

ski ski; skiing; **faire du ski** to go skiing

ski nautique waterskiing

slip pants

slip de bain swimming trunks

SMS text message

société company; society

sœur sister

soif thirst; **avoir soif** to be thirsty

soir evening; **ce soir** this evening, tonight; **le soir** in the evening(s)

soirée evening; party; **dans la soirée** in the evening

sol ground; floor

soldes sales; **en solde** in the sale

soleil sun; **au soleil** in the sun

sommeil sleep; **avoir sommeil** to be sleepy

sommet top, summit

somnifère sleeping pill

son his; her

sortie exit, way out

sortie de secours emergency exit

sortir to go out; to come out; **sortir avec quelqu'un** to go out with somebody; **sortir les poubelles** to take the rubbish out

souci worry; **se faire du souci (pour)** to worry (about)

souffrir to suffer

souhait wish; **à tes/vos souhaits !** bless you!

soûl drunk

sourd deaf

sourire (v) to smile; (n) smile

souris mouse
sous under
sous-titré subtitled
sous-vêtements underwear
soutien-gorge bra
souvenir memory; souvenir; **en souvenir de** in memory of; **se souvenir (de)** to remember
souvent often; **pas souvent** seldom
sparadrap sticking plaster
spécial special
spécialité speciality
spectacle show
sport sport
sportif sporty
stade stadium
standardiste (switchboard) operator
station balnéaire seaside resort
station de métro tube station
station de radio radio station
station de ski ski resort
station-service petrol station
stérilet coil
stop hitchhiking; **faire du stop** to hitchhike
stylo pen
succès success
sucre sugar
sucré sweet
sucreries sweet things
sud south; **au sud** in the south; **au sud de** (to the) south of
suffire to be enough; **ça suffit** that's enough
suivant next
suivre to follow; **faire suivre** to forward
super *(adj)* great
super *(n)* four-star petrol
supermarché supermarket
supplémentaire extra
supporter to put up with; **je ne supporte pas …** I can't stand …
sur on; over

sûr sure; **être sûr** to be sure; **bien sûr** of course
surf surfing; **faire du surf** to go surfing
surfer to surf
surprise surprise
surveiller to look after
sympa nice

T

ta your
tabac tobacco; tobacconist's
table table
tableau painting
tache stain
taie d'oreiller pillowcase
taille size; waist
tampon tampon
tant: tant mieux all the better; **tant pis** too bad
tante aunt
tapis rug
tapis de sol groundsheet
tard late; **à plus tard !** see you later!
tarif price, fare; **plein tarif** full price/ fare; **tarif réduit** concession
tasse cup, mug
taux de change exchange rate
taxe tax; **taxe d'aéroport** airport tax; **hors taxes** tax-free
taxi taxi
te you
tee-shirt T-shirt
télé TV
téléphone telephone
téléphone portable mobile (phone)
téléphoner (à) to (tele)phone
télésiège chairlift
télévision television
température temperature; **prendre sa température** to take one's temperature
tempête storm
temple temple; (Protestant) church

temporaire temporary
temps weather; time; **de temps en temps** from time to time; **tout le temps** all the time; **ces derniers temps** lately; **avoir le temps de** to have (the) time to
tenir to hold
tennis trainers
tension tension; stress; blood pressure
tente tent
terrain de camping campsite
terrain de golf golf course
terrain de sport sports ground
terrasse terrace; pavement area; **en terrasse** outside
terre earth; **par terre** on the ground/floor
tes your
tête head
théâtre theatre
thermomètre thermometer
ticket ticket
ticket de caisse receipt
tiède lukewarm
tien: le tien/la tienne yours; **les tiens/tiennes** yours
timbre stamp
timide shy
tire-bouchon corkscrew
tire-fesses T-bar
tirer to pull
tissu material
toi you
toilettes toilet; **toilettes pour hommes** gents'; **toilettes pour femmes** ladies'; **affaires de toilette** toiletries
tomber to fall; **tomber malade** to fall ill
ton your
tongs flip-flops
torchon dish towel
tôt early
toucher to touch

toujours always; still
touriste tourist
touristique tourist
tournée round
tourner to turn
tous all; **tous/toutes les deux** both; **tous les jours** every day
tousser to cough
tout all; **tout le temps** all the time; **tout le monde** everybody; **toute la journée** all day; **tout de suite** right away; **tout droit** straight ahead
toutes see **tous**
toux cough; **avoir de la toux** to have a cough
traditionnel traditional
traduire to translate
train train
tramway tram
tranche slice
tranquille quiet
transat deckchair
transpirer to sweat
travail work, job
travailler to work; **travailler dans** to work in
travaux works; roadworks
travers: à travers across
traverser to cross
très very
tromper: se tromper to make a mistake
trop too; too much; too many; **trop de** too much; too many
trou hole
trousse de toilette toilet bag
trouver to find; **trouver quelque chose difficile** to find something difficult
truc thing
tu you
tuer to kill
tupperware tupperware
TVA VAT

type type; guy

un, une a, an; one
Union européenne European Union
université university
urgence emergency; **en cas d'urgence** in an emergency; **appeler les urgences** to call the emergency services
urgent urgent
utile useful
utiliser to use

vacances holiday(s); **en vacances** on holiday
vacciner: être vacciné contre to be vaccinated against
vague wave
vaisselle dishes; **faire la vaisselle** to do the dishes
valable (pour) valid (for)
validité: en cours de validité valid
valise suitcase; **faire ses valises** to pack one's bags
vallée valley
valoir to be worth; **ça vaut ...** it's worth ...; **il vaut mieux ...** it's better to ...
végétarien vegetarian
vélo bike
vendeur shop assistant
vendre to sell; **à vendre** for sale
vendredi Friday
venir to come; **je viens de Paris** I come from Paris; **je viens d'arriver** I've just arrived
vent wind
ventilateur fan
ventre stomach
vérifier to check

verre glass; **verre d'eau/de vin** glass of water/of wine; **prendre un verre** to have a drink
verrou lock
vers towards
version: en version originale in the original language
vert green
veste jacket
vestiaire cloakroom
vêtement piece of clothing; **vêtements** clothes
vide empty
vie life
vieille old
vieux old; **les vieux** old people
village village
ville town; city; **vieille ville** old town
vin wine; **vin blanc/rouge** white/red wine
viol rape
violer to rape
violence violence
violent violent
violet purple
virement (bank) transfer
visa visa
visite visit; **rendre visite à ...** to visit ...
visite guidée guided tour
visiter to visit
vite fast, quickly
vitesse speed; **à toute vitesse** at full speed
vitraux stained-glass windows
vitre window
vitrine: en vitrine in the window
vivant living; alive
vivre to live
vœux: meilleurs vœux best wishes
voici here is/are
voilà there is/are
voile sail; sailing; **faire de la voile** to go sailing; **bateau à voile** sailing boat

voir to see
voisin neighbour
voiture car; coach; **en voiture** by car
voix voice; **à voix haute** aloud; **à voix basse** in a low voice
vol theft; flight
voler to steal; to fly
voleur thief
vomir to vomit; **avoir envie de vomir** to feel sick
vos your
votre your
vôtre: le/la vôtre yours; **les vôtres** yours
vouloir to want; **vouloir dire** to mean; **je voudrais …** I'd like …
vous you
voyage journey, trip; **bon voyage !** have a good trip!
voyage d'affaires business trip
voyage de noces honeymoon

voyage organisé package holiday
voyager to travel
voyelle vowel
vrai true; real
vraiment really
VTT mountain bike
vue view; **vue panoramique** panoramic view; **vue sur mer** sea view

---

WYZ

week-end weekend

y there; **il y a** there is/are
yeux eyes

zéro zero
zoo zoo
zoom zoom (lens)

GRAMMAR

French has two ways of saying *you* but these cover four situations: **polite** and **informal**, each in the singular and the plural. Use the informal form when speaking to friends or children, and the polite form to strangers, older people, or people in authority. In the singular, ie when you are speaking to just one person, the informal form is **tu** and the polite form is **vous**. The plural for both of these is **vous**, used when you are speaking to more than one person. So, when asking *how are you*:

	Singular	Plural
Informal	comment vas-tu ?	comment allez-vous ?
Polite	comment allez-vous ?	comment allez-vous ?

There are two ways of converting a statement into a **question** in French:
- by putting **est-ce que** (**est-ce qu'** when the first word of the statement starts with a vowel) in front of the statement:

>   leur mère habite en France *their mother lives in France*
>   est-ce que leur mère habite en France ? *does their mother live in France?*
>   est-ce qu'elle habite en France ? *does she live in France?*

- by inverting the verb and the subject and putting a hyphen between the two:

>   elle est à la maison *she's at home*
>   est-elle à la maison ? *is she at home?*
>   leur mère est à la maison *their mother's at home*
>   leur mère est-elle à la maison ? *is their mother at home?*

The first method is often easier to use than the second. In many situations, a statement can be turned into a question simply by using a rising intonation at the end of the statement:

>   leur mère habite en France ? *does their mother live in France?*

To make a sentence **negative**, insert **ne** (**n'** before a vowel) before the verb and **pas** after it:

>   Cécile vient demain *Cécile's coming tomorrow*
>   Cécile ne vient pas demain *Cécile's not coming tomorrow*

Negatives with *never* are formed with **ne** and **jamais**:

>   il n'appelle jamais *he never phones*

Negatives with *nothing/not anything* are formed with **ne** and **rien**:

> **je ne vois rien** I can see nothing, I can't see anything
> **elle n'a rien dit** she said nothing, she didn't say anything

French **nouns** are either **masculine** or **feminine**.

The **definite article** (*the* in English) and **indefinite article** (*a/an* in English) vary according to whether the noun is masculine or feminine, singular or plural:

	masc. sing.	masc. pl.	fem. sing.	fem. pl.
definite	le	les	la	les
indefinite	un	des	une	des

> **le garçon** the boy, **les garçons** the boys, **un garçon** a boy, **des garçons** some boys
> **la fille** the girl, **les filles** the girls, **une fille** a girl, **des filles** some girls

Note that **le** and **la** become **l'** before a word beginning with a vowel:

> **l'enfant** the child

The French for *some* is **du** in the masculine singular, **de la** in the feminine singular and **des** in the plural:

> **j'ai du vin** I've got some wine
> **j'ai de la glace** I've got some ice cream
> **j'ai des verres** I've got some glasses

In French a noun is virtually never used on its own without **le/la/les/du/de la/des** before it, so:

> **j'aime le vin blanc** I like white wine
> **j'aime les fraises** I like strawberries

In some case, the ending of a noun is a good indication of its **gender**.

- Words of more than one syllable with the following endings are generally masculine: **-age, -ail, -eau, -et, -isme, -ège, -ème, -ment**.
  le chauffage (heating), **le travail** (work), **le bateau** (boat), **le navet** (turnip), **le communisme** (communism), **le collège** (school), **le problème** (problem), **le vêtement** (garment)

- Words with the following endings are usually feminine: **-ance, -anse, -ion, -ine, -tte, -ure**.
  la tendance (tendency), **la danse** (dance), **la nation** (nation), **la cuisine** (kitchen, cooking), **la carotte** (carrot), **la nourriture** (food)

The **plural** of nouns is usually formed by adding **-s** as in English:
> table → **tables** (tables), chanson → **chansons** (songs)
> vélo → **vélos** (bikes), train → **trains** (trains)

Note that the final **-s** is not pronounced.
There are a number of exceptions:

- For nouns ending in **-au**, **-eau**, **-eu**, add **-x** to form the plural:
  des tuyaux (pipes), **des bateaux** (boats), **des neveux** (nephews)

- Some nouns ending in **-ou** also form the plural with **-x**:
  les genoux (knees), **des choux** (cabbages), **des bijoux** (jewels)

- For nouns ending in **-al**, the plural is usually formed by substituting **-aux** for **-al**:
  des journaux (newspapers), **des chevaux** (horses)

- Nouns ending in **-s**, **-z**, **-x** do not change in the plural:
  des radis (radishes), **les nez** (noses), **les prix** (prices)

Adjectives in French agree with nouns in number and gender and usually go *after* the noun:
> **un vin blanc** (a white wine), **deux vins blancs** (two white wines)
> **une rue étroite** (a narrow street), **des rues étroites** (narrow streets)

However, a few very common adjectives always go *before* the noun. These are:

> **bon/bonne** (good) – **un bon repas** (a good meal)
> **beau/belle** (beautiful, lovely) – **une belle maison** (a lovely house)
> **mauvais** (bad) – **du mauvais temps** (bad weather)
> **grand** (big, tall) – **un grand bâtiment** (a tall building)
> **gros/grosse** (big, large) – **une grosse somme** (a large sum)
> **petit** (small, little) – **un petit garçon** (a little boy)

The **plural** of adjectives is formed in the same way as for nouns. The **feminine** of adjectives is usually formed by adding **-e**:
> froid → **froide** (cold), chaud → **chaude** (hot)

There are exceptions which need to be learned individually but here are some patterns:

masc. ending	feminine	example
in **-c**	**-che**	blanc → blanche
in **-x**	**-se**	heureux → heureuse
in **-er**	**-ère**	léger → légère

| in -eau | -elle | beau → belle |
| in -ou | -olle | fou → folle |

Most **adverbs** are formed by adding **-ment** to the feminine form of the adjective:

lent (slow) → lentement (slowly)

Common adverbs not formed in this way are **bien** (well) and **mal** (badly).

Possessive adjectives (*my, your, his* etc) in French agree in number and gender with the noun that follows, unlike in English where they agree with the "possessor". For example:

he's lost *his* diary **il a perdu son** agenda (**agenda** is masculine)
she's lost *her* diary **elle a perdu son** agenda (**agenda** is masculine)
he's lost *his* keys **il a perdu ses clés** (**clés** is plural)
she's lost *her* keys **elle a perdu ses clés** (**clés** is plural)

Shown below are the masculine, feminine and plural forms for each:

my	**mon, ma, mes**
your[1]	**ton, ta, tes**
his/her/its	**son, sa, ses**
our	**notre, notre, nos**
your[2]	**votre, votre, vos**
their	**leur, leur, leurs**

[1] Informal, talking to one person.

[2] Talking to more than one person or to one person you do not know well.

The **subject pronouns** (*I, you, we* etc) are as follows:

je (I)	**nous** (we)
tu (you[1])	**vous** (you[2])
il (he, it[3]), **elle** (she, it[3])	**ils, elles** (they[3])

[1] Informal, talking to one person.

[2] Talking to more than one person or to one person you do not know well.

[3] Depending on the gender in French of who or what is being referred to.

French distinguishes between direct object pronouns (I like *them*) and indirect object pronouns (I gave *them* the address = I gave the address *to them*).

The **direct object pronouns** (*me, you* etc) are as follows:

me (me)	**nous** (us)
te (you[1])	**vous** (you[2])
le (him, it[3]), **la** (her, it[3])	**les** (them)

[1] Informal talking to one person.

[2] Talking to more than one person or to one person you do not know well.

[3] Depending on the gender in French of what is being referred to.

Note that **me**, **te**, **le/la** become **m'**, **t'**, **l'** before a word beginning with a vowel.

> **il m'a vu** he saw me
>
> **je t'appellerai ce soir** I'll ring you tonight

The **indirect object pronouns** (*(to) me, (to) you* etc) are as follows:

me (me)	**nous** (us)
te (you[1])	**vous** (you[2])
lui (him, her, it)	**leur** (them)

[1] Informal, talking to one person.

[2] Talking to more than one person or to one person you do not know well.

> **elle lui a envoyé une carte** she sent him/her a card
>
> **je leur ai donné mon adresse** I gave them my address

Possessive pronouns are the words we use to say who something belongs to: this is *mine* and that's *yours*. French adds the information on the gender and number of what it is that belongs to the person.

> **le mien/la mienne/les miens/miennes** (mine)
>
> **le tien/la tienne/les tiens/les tiennes** (yours[1])
>
> **le sien/la sienne/les siens/les siennes** (his, hers, its[3])
>
> **le/la nôtre/les nôtres** (ours)
>
> **le/la vôtre/les vôtres** (yours[2])
>
> **le/la leur/les leurs** (theirs)

[1] Informal talking to one person.

[2] Talking to more than one person or to one person you do not know well.

[3] Depending on the gender in French of who or what is being referred to.

Note that people will often prefer to say: **c'est à moi/à toi/à eux** (it's mine/yours/theirs) to indicate possession. These are called **disjunctive pronouns**. They are used after prepositions and in statements like **c'est moi !** (it's me!). The disjunctive pronouns are:

moi (me, I)	**nous** (we, us)
toi (you)	**vous** (you)
lui (him, he, it), **elle** (her, she, it)	**eux, elles** (them, they)

> **c'est pour toi** it's for you
>
> **les verres sont à eux** the glasses are theirs
>
> **moi, je crois que ...** I think that ...

Reflexive pronouns are used when the subject and the object of the verb are identical: I saw *myself* in the mirror. In French these are:

me (myself)	**nous** (ourselves)
te (yourself[1])	**vous** (yourselves[2])
se (himself, herself, itself)	**se** (themselves)

[1] Informal, talking to one person.
[2] Talking to more than one person or to one person you do not know well.
Note that **te** and **se** become **t'** and **s'** before a word beginning with a vowel.

> **il s'est blessé** he's hurt *himself*

In French some verbs that carry an idea of doing something to oneself are **reflexive verbs**, so are used with a reflexive pronoun. These are shown in the dictionary section. Examples are:

> **je me réveille** I wake up
> **je me lève** I get up

French **verbs** are divided into three groups (conjugations), ending in -**er**, -**ir** and -**re**.
Here is the **present tense** of three regular verbs, one from each conjugation. A hyphen has been inserted only so that you can see the endings more clearly:

parler	**finir**	**attendre**
je parl-**e**	je fin-**is**	j'attend-**s**
tu parl-**es**	tu fin-**is**	tu attend-**s**
il/elle parl-**e**	il/elle fin-**it**	il/elle attend
nous parl-**ons**	nous fin-**issons**	nous attend-**ons**
vous parl-**ez**	vous fin-**issez**	vous attend-**ez**
ils/elles parl-**ent**	ils/elles fin-**issent**	ils/elles attend-**ent**

vous parlez très bien français you speak very good French
ils finissent leur repas they're finishing their meal
je t'attends dehors I'll wait for you outside

There are also a number of irregular verbs which have to be learnt. Here are some common irregular verbs in the present tense:

être[1] (to be)	**avoir**[1] (to have)	**aller** (to go)
je suis	j'ai	je vais
tu es	tu as	tu vas
il/elle est	il/elle a	il/elle va
nous sommes	nous avons	nous allons

| vous êtes | vous avez | vous allez |
| ils/elles sont | ils/elles ont | ils/elles vont |

faire (to do)	**venir** (to come)	**dire** (to say)
je fais	je viens	je dis
tu fais	tu viens	tu dis
il/elle fait	il/elle vient	il/elle dit
nous faisons	nous venons	nous disons
vous faites	vous venez	vous dites
ils/elles font	ils/elles viennent	ils/elles disent

devoir (to have to)	**pouvoir** (to come)	**vouloir** (to want)
je dois	je peux	je veux
tu dois	tu peux	tu veux
il/elle doit	il/elle peut	il/elle veut
nous devons	nous pouvons	nous voulons
vous devez	vous pouvez	vous voulez
ils/elles doivent	ils/elles peuvent	ils/elles veulent

mettre (to put)	**voir** (to see)	**savoir** (to know)
je mets	je vois	je sais
tu mets	tu vois	tu sais
il/elle met	il/elle voit	il/elle sait
nous mettons	nous voyons	nous savons
vous mettez	vous voyez	vous savez
ils/elles mettent	ils/elles voient	ils/elles savent

¹ **Être** and **avoir** are also used as *auxiliary verbs* when forming the **present perfect** tense.

Avoir is used for most verbs:

    j'**ai** acheté un pantalon I've bought some trousers

    as-tu vu ce film ? have you seen this film?

Être is used to form the present perfect tense of verbs of motion and change of state:

    elle **est** allée* au cinéma she's gone to the cinema

    ils **sont** venus* ici l'année dernière they came here last year

*Note that when a verb forms its present perfect with **être**, the past participle agrees in gender and number with the subject of the verb.

The **imperfect** tense is used to express a continuous action in the past (eg I *was talking* to him). Here is how to form the imperfect tense for regular verbs:

parler	finir	attendre
je parl-**ais**	je fin-**issais**	j'attend-**ais**
tu parl-**ais**	tu fin-**issais**	tu attend-**ais**
il/elle parl-**ait**	il/elle fin-**issait**	il/elle attend-**ait**
nous parl-**ions**	nous fin-**issions**	nous attend-**ions**
vous parl-**iez**	vous fin-**issiez**	vous attend-**iez**
ils/elles parl-**aient**	ils/elles fin-**issaient**	ils/elles attend-**aient**

The imperfect of **être** is: j'étais, tu étais, il/elle était, nous étions, vous étiez, ils/elles étaient.

The imperfect of **avoir** is: j'avais, tu avais, il/elle avait, nous avions, vous aviez, ils/elles avaient.

The **future** tense is usually formed by adding the following endings to the infinitive:

-ai, **-as**, **-a**, **-ons**, **-ez**, **-ont**

Example with **parler**: je parlerai, tu parleras, il/elle parlera, nous parlerons, vous parlerez, ils/elles parleront.

> je lui parlerai demain I'll talk to him/her tomorrow
> le match finira à 17h the match will finish at 5pm

HOLIDAYS AND FESTIVALS

NATIONAL BANK HOLIDAYS

In France, bank holidays are known as **jours fériés**. Administrative offices, banks, offices and most shops are closed.

1 January	**le jour de l'an**, also known as **le nouvel an** (New Year's Day)
March/April	**lundi de Pâques** (Easter Monday)
1 May	**le premier mai**, **fête du travail** (Labour Day)
8 May	**le 8 mai** (VE Day, celebrating the end of the German occupation of France in the Second World War)
May	**le jeudi de l'Ascension** (Ascension)
14 July	**le 14 juillet** (French National Day, celebrating the storming of the Bastille in 1789)
15 August	**l'Assomption** (Assumption)
1 November	**la Toussaint** (All Saints' Day)
11 November	**le 11 novembre**, also known as **l'Armistice** (Armistice Day, celebrating the end of the First World War)
25 December	**Noël** (Christmas Day)

FESTIVALS

The French love festivals. Every village holds its own, mainly during the summer months. There are also numerous cultural festivals held throughout the year.

January	Some town and villages still celebrate **carnival** but the custom is no longer widespread. A notable exception is the northern city of Dunkirk where celebrations and parades are held from 24 January until 13 March.
February	Another internationally known carnival is held in Nice, on the Mediterranean coast. Some of the traditions include the Battle of the Flowers parade, the **carnastring** (a dip in the Baie des Anges on the first Sunday of the festival) and the **carnacourse**, a race for waiters in which they can show off their tray-carrying skills. And of course there are the traditional parades and fireworks.

| May | The **Festival international du film de Cannes** is without doubt the most important cinematic event in the world. Every year a whole host of stars descend on the Mediterranean resort. The winning film is awarded the prestigious **palme d'or** (golden palm) award. |

June
A major national event is the **Festival de la musique** which is held on 21 June, the first day of summer and is celebrated in town and villages all over the country. Every type of music has its place, from classical to rock, reggae and folk. Events are publicized well in advance and range from gala concerts in prestigious venues to an endless variety of street music.

On **la Saint-Jean** (Midsummer's Day: 24 June) it is the custom in many areas to light bonfires. Traditionally people jump over these in order to prevent the winter's cold from returning.

July
Another major cultural event takes place every year in Avignon, the seat of the Pope in the 14th century and situated on the banks of the Rhone. The **Festival d'Avignon** features music, dance and open-air theatre. The official programme is accompanied by the "**off**" festival, seen as a springboard for young talent.

A major French sporting event is the **Tour de France**. For the three weeks of the race the whole country is gripped, with passions running high. Whenever the cyclists pass through a town or village, everything stops and a real party atmosphere breaks out.

14 July
The French national day is a celebration of the storming of the Bastille prison (**la prise de la Bastille**) in 1789, during the French Revolution. It is the most important festival of the year, and even the tiniest villages put on a **bal** (dance) and firework displays.

November
La fête du beaujolais is celebrated each year on 18 November, the date on which the year's new vintage, **le beaujolais nouveau**, comes onto the market. The beaujolais wine-growing region lies just to the north of Lyons. Cafés and restaurants all over the country put on festive events at which the new wine can be sampled and a big celebration is held in the region's capital, Villefranche-sur-Saône.

USEFUL ADDRESSES

IN FRANCE

British Embassy
35, rue du Faubourg Saint-Honoré 70008 Paris
Tel: 01 44 51 31 00

There are British Consulates in the other four big cities in France. If you have a problem, you should contact the nearest one. The telephone numbers are:

Bordeaux: 05 57 22 21 10   Lille: 03 20 12 82 72
Lyon: 04 72 77 81 70   Marseille: 04 91 15 72 10

Irish Embassy
4, rue Rude 75016 Paris
Tel: 01 44 17 67 00

Tourist Information – Paris
127, avenue des Champs-Élysées 75008 Paris
Tel: 01 49 52 53 54

IN THE UK

French Embassy – London
58, Knightsbridge London SW1X 7JT
Tel: 0207 073 1000

French Tourist Office – London
178, Piccadilly London W1J 9AL
Tel: 0207 499 6911

CONVERSION TABLES

Note that when writing numbers, French uses a comma where English uses a full stop. For example 2.5 would be written 2,5 in French and spoken as *deux virgule cinq*.

Measurements

Only the metric system is used in France.

Length
1 cm ≈ 0.4 inches
30 cm ≈ 1 foot

Distance
1 metre ≈ 1 yard
1 km ≈ 0.6 miles

To convert kilometres into miles, divide by 8 and then multiply by 5.

kilometres	1	2	5	10	20	100
miles	0.6	1.25	3.1	6.25	12.50	62.5

To convert miles into kilometres, divide by 5 and then multiply by 8.

miles	1	2	5	10	20	100
kilometres	1.6	3.2	8	16	32	160

Weight
25g ≈ 1 oz   1 kg ≈ 2 lb   6 kg ≈ 1 stone

To convert kilos into pounds, divide by 5 and then multiply by 11.
To convert pounds into kilos, multiply by 5 and then divide by 11.

kilos	1	2	10	20	60	80
pounds	2.2	4.4	22	44	132	176

Liquid
1 litre ≈ 2 pints
4.5 litres ≈ 1 gallon

Temperature

To convert temperatures in Celsius into Fahrenheit, divide by 5, multiply by 9 and then add 32.

To convert temperatures in Fahrenheit into Celsius, subtract 32, multiply by 5 and then divide by 9.

Celsius (°C)	0	4	10	15	20	30	38
Fahrenheit (°F)	32	40	50	59	68	86	100

Clothes sizes

Sometimes you will find sizes given using the English-language abbreviations **XS**, **S**, **M**, **L** and **XL** and often, as in the UK, sizes from 1 to 4. Otherwise, see below:

• Women's clothes

Europe	36	38	40	42	44	etc
UK	8	10	12	14	16	

• Bras (cup sizes are the same)

Europe	70	75	80	85	90	etc
UK	32	34	36	38	40	

• Men's shirts (collar size)

Europe	36	38	41	43	etc
UK	14	15	16	17	

• Men's clothes

Europe	40	42	44	46	48	50 etc
UK	30	32	34	36	38	40

Shoe sizes

• Women's shoes

Europe	37	38	39	40	42	etc
UK	4	5	6	7	8	

• Men's shoes

Europe	40	42	43	44	46	etc
UK	7	8	9	10	11	